EXODUS TO THE

VIRTUAL WORLD

How Online Fun Is Changing Reality

Edward Castronova

First published in 2007 by
PALGRAVE MACMILLAN™
175 Fifth Avenue, New York, N.Y. 10010 and
Houndmills, Basingstoke, Hampshire, England RG21 6XS.
Companies and representatives throughout the world.

PALGRAVE MACMILLAN is the global academic imprint of the Palgrave
Macmillan division of St. Martin's Press, LLC and of Palgrave Macmillan Ltd.
Macmillan® is a registered trademark in the United States, United Kingdom
and other countries. Palgrave is a registered trademark in the European Union
and other countries.

ISBN–13: 978–1–4039–8412–8
ISBN–10: 1–4039–8412–3

Library of Congress Cataloging-in-Publication Data

Castronova, Edward.
    Exodus to the virtual world : how online fun is changing reality / by Edward
Castronova.
    p.   cm.
    ISBN 1–4039–8412–3 (alk. paper)
    1. Internet games—Social aspects.   2. Virtual reality—Social aspects.
3. Fantasy games—Social aspects.   4. Civilization, Modern—21st century—
Forecasting.   I. Title.
    GV1469.15.C393   2007
    793.93'2—dc22

                                                          2007014272

A catalogue record of the book is available from the British Library.

Design by Letra Libre, Inc.

First edition: December 2007

10 9 8 7 6 5 4 3 2 1

Printed in the United States of America.

For Luca and Malcolm

CONTENTS

ACKNOWLEDGMENTS

This book started out as a more academic piece about video games and public policy. Then I got a call from the fellow who's become my agent, Andrew Stuart, who helped me realize that this subject needs vision before we can do analysis. Thanks for that, and for encouragement along the way. The latter was especially needed when Amanda Moon, my editor at Palgrave, made me aware of how very plodding writing can be. Through her help I have been able to flush out many torpor-inducing conditionals, hesitations, subjunctives, academic setups, and pedantic conclusions. Unfortunately, even a person of her great skills could not stop the flood of grammar krill I sent at her; many thousands of bad words remain. I thank her for trying.

Indiana University graduate student James Cummings read the book in an early form and gave helpful comments and discussions along the way. My department chair, the always gracious and patient Walter Gantz, covered for me when work on the book meant I couldn't do other things. The university itself has been a fabulous place to work on books and video games. It's been very good to be a Hoosier. I recommend it.

The people who bore the brunt of the pain the writing of this book has caused, however, are once again members of my family. I bitterly recall writing in the preface to my first book that I would forevermore spend all of my time at home. Ha. Here I am, writing another preface. This treadmill is very hard to jump off. But I am going to try it again. I want to spend time with my wife, Nina, and my sons, Luca and Malcolm, now, when we are all young and strong and full of energy and life.

It's funny. The biggest risk to my family time is not video gaming. You'd think it would be—I'm a video game scholar, it's clear I love games and want to play them all the time. Everybody *knows* that video games make you a nerd who sits in your mom's basement eating pizza and avoiding all contact with girls. Right? No. Not right. When we play games at our home, we play them together. The thing that makes me a nerd, that makes me eat pizza and avoid all thought of girls and love and life and family isn't games, it's *work*. Everybody may *know* that work is good and games are bad. But everybody can be wrong, too.

That's one of the reasons I wrote this book. Many think video games push people toward an unhealthy lifestyle. I think the lifestyles of the real world are already unhealthy, and that large-scale social video games will expose us to alternative social orders, some of which will be much better than anything we have now. I'm sick of the way that the real world pulls families apart, the way it makes people give their time to huge soulless organizations rather than themselves, the way it deadens our willingness to be mature about right and wrong, the way it isolates us and takes away all sense of personal meaning and significance. Synthetic worlds already address many of those problems, without even knowing or trying. From where I sit, it's no wonder at all that video game worlds are as attractive as they are to so many people. The lesson is that we should look at what these worlds are doing, to see what aspects of lost human experience they have rediscovered, then try to rebuild those things in the real world.

ACKNOWLEDGMENTS

That's a global quest, but like many good quests it starts at home. One of the lost pleasures that virtual worlds have rediscovered is that of community. I want community with my own family. This time I mean it. Work doesn't matter. I want to be with you, Nina, and with you, Luca, and you, Malcolm. Thank you for giving me the time and space I needed to finish this project. It's done. Now we can be together a lot more. We can do lots of things. Let's play some games!

PREFACE

This is a work of speculative nonfiction. Professors are generally discouraged from writing books like this. Ordinarily, speculation is supposed to play no role in what we do. Generally, our job is to explain things that are, not predict things to come. Prediction is guesswork; what we're supposed to be doing is not guessing about things but rather developing theories about how the world really works and then verifying those theories against experience. There's not supposed to be much guesswork in that. If anything, we are supposed to be fighting to reduce guesswork, to give people in business, government, education, and families—people for whom guesswork is an unavoidable and unpleasant part of the job—some foundation of accepted knowledge. We're supposed to help provide a basis of known things that will make the necessary job of deciding what to do a little bit easier.

At times, however, a professor finds himself called to write something outside the usual lines, something that involves a mix of experience and visioning. Scientists who learn how things work today occasionally also develop opinions about how the systems they've discovered are going to operate in the future. At times, those future operations will involve big changes. The climatologists who came to understand the role of carbon dioxide in global temperatures knew how those systems interacted, and that was science. When they then surmised that rising global temperatures could dramatically affect human life, it wasn't exactly science any more. The further thought that humans were producing CO_2 in historically unprecedented levels (and therefore might be at fault for the temperature changes that would dramatically affect them) was moving even farther from the science of climatology. And finally, when the scientists began to speak out about the future they felt might be coming, that was not science at all, but a form of public visioning. Generally, scientists are not supposed to be public advocates for anything. But when a scientist has seen an ongoing process that might dramatically affect how others live, and it seems that the sooner people know about it the better off everyone will be, public visioning becomes an appropriate role. The climatologists were called to speak out about global warming, not in their role as scientists, but in their role as human beings. Anyone who sees a hurricane coming should warn others.

I see a hurricane coming. It's called practical virtual reality. In my book *Synthetic Worlds*, I explain that practical virtual reality is not scientific virtual reality, launched in the 1990s, which involves head-mounted displays and laboratory rooms with video projectors and surround sound. That research continues today, productively I assume. Practical virtual reality emerged unannounced from the dark imagineering labs of the video game industry, got powered by high-speed Internet connections, and exploded across the globe, catching us all by surprise. Already, practical virtual reality immerses 20 or 30 million people in worlds of perpetual fantasy. Over the next generation or two, hundreds of millions more will join them.

The exodus of these people from the real world, from our normal daily life of living rooms, cubicles, and shopping malls, will create a change in social climate that makes global warming look like a tempest in a teacup. Their exodus might be your exodus. Many of us will find ourselves interacting in cyberspace much of the time. Perhaps you will be a sexy warrior, and I will be a wayward monk. Or you will be riding your Harley, and I will be driving my Mustang. Or you will be performing at Carnegie Hall, and I will be watching you in my ravishing evening gown. Or you will be orbiting Alpha Centauri, and I will be seeking you with my deep-space sensors. Or you will be a writer of speculative nonfiction, and I will be a presidential candidate trying to see the future. Whatever our deepest shared fantasies may be, we will be able to pursue them in cyberspace together, all day, every day, world without end.

In virtual reality we will be playing, not working, but I think our play will actually be generating a moderate income for us, enough to offset some of the (low) cost of play. In playing we will make durable things that can be sold to other players. We will develop skills that others will pay us to perform. Sometimes, that game income will be a source of value that can pay for things we will always need in the real world—housing, food. More often, that game income will go toward game expenses. I will blacksmith for you and use the money to buy a virtual horse from Jim (or Galahad, as he is known in the fantasy world). Galahad will use the money from his horse to buy tailoring equipment, which gives Guenevere the virtual money she needs for passage on a virtual ship owned by Edmund the Sea-Captain—who is named Hailey in real life. Our demands will be largely virtual, and so will the supplies; production, consumption, and income. We will all spend time in virtual reality just because we can. It doesn't take a lot of resources to keep a body alive, and the mind will be having a good time.

The biggest effect of all of this play, I think, will not be on us but rather on the outside world. While we are playing, things we used to do on the outside, in "reality," won't be happening any more, or won't be happening in the same way. You can't pull millions of person-hours out of a society without creating an atmospheric-level event. There will be change. There may be disruption, depending on how rapidly all those hours slip away. If it happens in a generation, I think the twenty-first century will see a social cataclysm larger than that caused by cars, radios, and TV, combined, in the twentieth.

How could it not be? If someone built a persistent virtual reality environment where you could be anything you wanted to be, all the time, wouldn't you go there? At least for a while every day? And if you think you wouldn't, how about other people? Maybe your life is good. Maybe you're a successful business person. An actor. A happily married parent with two nice kids. Maybe you've got a degree from an elite school and you're well on your way to the top. Maybe you're a presidential candidate. But how many people can only fantasize about the life you have? For each happy, fulfilled person, how many are there who are bored, frustrated, unappreciated, defeated, unhappy? There's quite a lot of self-medication going on. Whatever people learn in school, it doesn't seem to be leading to stable homes, happy childhoods, and emotionally grounded adult lives. In some cases, sure. But in my view, there are quite a lot of people who crave change, and virtual reality can make their lives different: more exciting, more rewarding, more heroic, more meaningful. And those people, quite rationally, will spend much of their time in the virtual worlds now exploding onto the scene.

You and I may or may not join them in this choice. Regardless, their exodus, because of its sheer size, will affect us all. The idea that millions of people will start living out their fantasies inside huge computer games is understandably unsettling. Currently, the public's reaction to video games in general seems marked by no small amount of terror. But the situation is not completely unknowable. I am hoping that some informed prediction, with some nuts and bolts along the way, might calm our nerves a bit.

I predict the following:

1. Ever larger numbers of people will spend many hours inside on-line games. To the rest of us, these choices will feel like an exodus from our reality. Our reality will be changed.

2. As an effect of this exodus, the public at large will come to think of game design and public policy design as roughly similar activities. This is because, structurally, they are the same. They both involve assessing the interests of large numbers of otherwise unassociated people, and then determining the best course of action for the authorities (government in one case, game developers in the other).

3. Because of these similarities, there will be crossovers in know-how. In *Synthetic Worlds* I described how real-world policy analysis could be used to help game design. In this book, I discuss how some techniques that game designers have discovered and successfully used may find their way into real-world policy debates.

4. While all of this is happening, we will also have to come to a new and more rigorous understanding of human happiness. Games are designed to make people happy. As the lines between public policy and game design blur, public policy will begin to focus more directly on human happiness, even fun, than it does now. Ultimately, games will force fun onto the policy agenda.

I focus on public policy primarily because we understand how it operates fairly well. We can see the analytical logic behind public policy predictions more easily than, say, the equally (and probably more) important impact of virtual reality on the family. This book tries to focus on predictions that proceed from the nuts and bolts of certain specific models in economics and public policy.

The models I am using here—the nuts and bolts of my prediction machine—include:

1. The likely development of game technology in the next few decades.
2. Human migration and its economic, social, and public policy effects.
3. The economic theory of human time use, and the allocation of attention.
4. The psychology of human happiness, and more specifically, the sensations people get when they play digital games.
5. The tools public policy analysis uses for questions of happiness.

It's necessary to put some concrete foundations under what is, in the end, an exercise in visioning. Since the vision might seem surprising, it helps to know that it is an extension of some fairly well-trod intellectual ground.

I've limited myself to thinking only one or two generations into the future—20–40 years. I imagine much of what's discussed in these pages will happen long before then. But it is just too easy to insist that the revolution is right around the corner. The millenarian impulse is strong. You, the reader, however, should understand that I don't particularly care how rapidly any of this happens. And so I'm content to be conservative and say that some sort of major social change will happen as we move toward a population where the vast majority is familiar with virtual reality from childhood. That would take 40 years. But for all I know, it could happen by the time this book hits the stores. Change will come. Computing power will turn the Internet into a vast universe of fantasy realms, and millions of us will head off into the haze. We can only guess how rapidly it is happening.[1]

The full effect of the virtual world exodus will only become clear as time passes. But we can and should start getting ready for the more obvious things right now. Therefore, a book of informed speculation, whose language is academic and cautious yet whose message is fire and brimstone. For better or worse, it's being written by an economist who has taught public policy at the university level for more than a decade. He's also logged thousands of hours inside contemporary virtual worlds and watched their growth closely. He's in his forties, not his twenties; married, two kids; doesn't completely understand his cell phone. All he really knows, professionally speaking, is what every economist knows: When something entertaining appears at an affordable price, people go for it in droves. Only this time, "buying" the product means disappearing from daily life for hours and hours at a time. It means spending whole weekends and every night until 2 A.M. logged into a computer-driven fantasy world. In previous work, I analyzed the people who logged in. Now, I'm reporting my impressions of how their behavior, as it becomes widespread, will affect everyone else. The virtual world has been discovered; the new frontier shimmers on the horizon, plain to see. We need to start talking about what that means, for all of us.

PART ONE

NEW FOUND LAND

CHAPTER ONE

DREAMS FASHIONED IN SILICON

THE HOLODECK IS HERE

A *holodeck* is a perfect simulation room, a science fiction fantasy from the TV show *Star Trek: The Next Generation*. As conceived there, the holodeck allows users to enter into a deeply accurate simulation of any environment, from the Wild West to the surface of Pluto. Moreover, the holodeck can be populated with simulated people who are just as realistic as their virtual environments. On the TV show, these holodecks are for training and occasional entertainment: Characters use them to practice Klingon fighting moves, or to solve Agatha Christie mysteries. According to the scripts, when the training (and fun) is over, the real people go back to their "real" work of maintaining and operating a starship. The writers, no doubt catering to their sense of what the audience expects, apparently believe that if a holodeck existed, it would be used like a super-duper but serious TV: Mostly for mild entertainment, but occasionally for working on mental and physical skills; the same mix of sitcoms, training videos, and exercise programs, but super-duper.

As an economist, I have always been puzzled by this mild conception of the holodeck's effect on the Star Trek crew. Economists generally argue that people will pursue as long as possible activities that please them. If Activity A is more pleasant than Activity B, but has the same cost in terms of money and time, Activity A will be chosen first. A person only switches to Activity B when Activity A gets too boring or too expensive. This is the basic economic theory of time allocation, described first by Nobel Laureate Gary Becker almost a half century ago and since confirmed by reams of empirical evidence. And according to this theory, the crew's use of the holodeck is going to be driven by how entertaining the holodeck is, relative to other activities, and how expensive it is to use. It seems to me that a holodeck, on the Starship *Enterprise* or anywhere else, would be an almost infinitely entertaining toy. Remember, it is said to be programmable to produce *any scene desired*, including other people. The holodeck seems available to every crew member, free of charge. An infinitely pleasing toy, for free. Considering such an object, the question is not why people spend time with it, but rather why people spend time doing anything else. Why isn't every single crewmember in the holodeck, all the time? If the technology truly existed as described, economics clearly predicts that all crew members would program the holodeck to produce their most desired fantasy existence, and then disappear into it.

But if all crew members are in the holodeck, no one will be running the ship. If you put a holodeck on every starship, no starship would ever report back to base; indeed, *no starship would do anything at all.*

Now imagine what the world would look like if someone invented and marketed a holodeck not for starships, but for every home. This scenario has moved from the realm of nerdy speculation to that of practical policy. A new technology has emerged, in just the last five years, that is shockingly close to a holodeck. Already today, a person with a reasonably well-equipped personal computer and an Internet connection can disappear for hours and hours into vast realms of fantasy. These computer-generated virtual worlds are unquestionably the holodeck's predecessors. This technology will draw in millions and millions of people, and many of them will indeed dramatically reduce the amount of time they spend doing things in the real world. These developments, which will take place over the next one or two generations, will probably not bring our "starships" to a grinding halt, but they will alter patterns of daily life in a significant way.

This technology is known as *virtual worlds* (or more precisely, *synthetic worlds*): massive multiuser online environments where millions of people live out a collective fantasy existence.[1] It is not hard to do. Right now, you could put down this book, go to your local store, and buy *Lord of the Rings Online* by the game development company Turbine, Inc. After setting up the software (including agreeing to a monthly fee of about $10 to $15), the character you've created, an *avatar*, will enter a synthetic rendition of J.R.R. Tolkien's Middle Earth. Looking around, you'll see a beautiful landscape with trees, grass, birds, rabbits, lakes, and little cottages. You'll also see lots of other characters, some being run by the system's artificial intelligence engines, others by people just like you. Press the "Enter" key and type a sentence; what you wrote is transmitted to everyone else in your vicinity just as if you were in a crowded room and had spoken the sentence aloud. The people in the world will now react to you as well, asking you what you meant, what you want, where you are going. That quickly, you are virtual worlding. You've gone off to the virtual frontier.[2]

Access to these experiences is growing rapidly. *World of Warcraft*, by Blizzard Entertainment, launched in 2004 and quickly acquired one

CARLA: ENTREPRENEUR

Our story's hypothetical protagonist is Carla, a 35-year-old unmarried white-collar worker with no children. She spends her days managing the office of a car dealership, her nights online in a 3D environment called *Second Life,* produced and managed by the Silicon Valley company Linden Labs, Inc. In *Second Life (SL),* Carla has chosen a body that looks quite a bit prettier than her real body, but that sort of choice has been amply studied by previous Internet researchers.[4] What's new is that Carla is also a producer and an entrepreneur in the virtual world. *SL* has a production technology that allows users to build whatever they want—rockets, talking flowers, bizarre hairdos, and so on. The way it works is simple: In a dialogue box you can click on various options to create simple objects. You can then combine them into more complex objects. You could make a table out of one flat rectangle and four tall rectangles. If you can write code-like instructions, you can make even more complex things, from huge buildings to facial dimples. Using this production technology, Carla can make things in *SL.* The production technologies in other worlds don't give you this kind of freedom, but every single one of them does allow you to convert raw materials you find in the world into more complex objects. Every synthetic world has a production economy, a supply side to its markets.

Carla can sell the things she makes to other people, because *SL* has a currency, Linden dollars. This again is not hard. She can build a store to house her wares and automated vendors to conclude transactions. She can make billboards that advertise her store's location. Let's say she makes dresses. People will come to her store because they see nice-looking characters and ask, "Where did you get that dress?" In other words, the market in *SL* works like that in real life: word of mouth, reputation, craftsmanship, fair dealing, honest prices. And these market and business conditions are the same in every synthetic world, although again not with the same degree of freedom as *SL* affords. In a game like *World of Warcraft*, you cannot make just *anything*, as you can in *Second Life*. But you can make one of hundreds of thousands of things, using specific recipes, and then you can sell them using a synthetic currency. Your business acumen will matter. If you do well, like Carla, you will soon acquire a mass of virtual currency.

What then? What does one do with a virtual fortune? One option is to spend it on virtual things. Carla might want to buy an *SL* mansion that someone else has built, rather than spend all the hours to build it herself. But another option would be to liquidate the virtual fortune by turning it into real money. Carla can easily do that. Linden Labs provides a currency exchange market called the Lindex, where people who want to sell Linden dollars meet people who want to buy them. It runs a lot like eBay—anonymous buyers and sellers use a reputation system to choose whom they want to deal with, and all transactions are concluded electronically: Your Linden dollars go into my *SL* account, and my real dollars go into your real bank account. In case there's any doubt, yes, people do want to buy Linden dollars. If you buy Linden dollars by the truckload, you don't have to build anything in *SL*—you just buy the things other people have built. You could move into a mansion on your first day. While some people enjoy *SL* for the joy of construction, many more just want to play out an alternate reality, assuming a wildly different body type, a flashy car or spaceship, and a big mansion. Such people are more than willing to spend $10 or $50 in real money to get a really sexy character or a really big swimming pool. These folks will buy Carla's surplus Linden dollars, allowing her to turn her virtual fortune into a modest real income.

This is where things get interesting to an outsider. Let's say Carla's hours in *SL* result in about $1,200 monthly in real income. Carla, being a low-level white-collar worker, might have a take-home pay from her real job of $1,800 monthly. Carla's total productive contribution to the economy, measured by the amount of money that other people are willing to pay her, is worth $3,000. But 40 percent of it occurs in a synthetic environment. What does this mean for the economy as a whole? The number we use to measure economic activity for a whole economy is the gross domestic product (GDP): the total value of goods and services produced. So, fine, we add Carla's $3,000 to GDP, noting merely that 40 percent of it came from online production. But what about the things she made in *SL* but *did not cash out?* She made a lot of Linden dollars that she never sold for real dollars. Do they count in GDP as well?

There's no right answer. When we unpack "GDP" into "gross *domestic* product," some revolutionary thoughts come to mind. What's the domicile here to which *domestic* refers? Is *SL* part of America? If so, then we ought to be counting all of Carla's *SL* production as part of U.S. GDP. It was produced in America and it was sold in America. Sure, some of it was sold for Linden dollars, but that doesn't matter. If I pick cherries from my orchard and give them to you for honey from your honeybees, it's barter, not a money transaction, but it still counts as production (not to mention taxes). All of Carla's production counts. Well, that notion is going to unsettle lots of people when they first hear it—"You mean, somebody goes into a video game and makes flowers, and we're supposed to count that in GDP?"

If we go the other way and declare that Carla's *SL* production is *not* part of the U.S. economy, we have just decreed that every minute that Carla spends producing in the synthetic economy is lost to U.S. GDP.

Now imagine a future in which most Americans spend a good fraction of their time in synthetic worlds, and a lot of what they do involves making virtual things for sale or trade to others. (That's an extremely likely future, but we will get to that a little later.) Let's say the American economy ends up working like Carla does—60 percent of production in the real world, 40 percent in virtual worlds. Think about how GDP will evolve as we move from the current situation to this likely future situation. Today, 100 percent of economic production is in the real world. In the future, only 60 percent will be. If we do not count virtual-world production as part of GDP, then our GDP measurement will fall by 40 percent as this future unfolds. That fall would be equivalent to the decline in GDP during the Great Depression. And GDP is not the only thing that would fall. If we declare that the *SL* economy is separate from our own, the IRS gets no sales tax from transactions there. No income tax on virtual earnings. No Social Security contributions. No Medicare contributions. No unemployment insurance contributions. The real world would perceive this as a severe economic collapse, and the power and influence of government would wane considerably.

This is not the place to argue whether that would be good or bad. The point is that the changes about to be imposed by the looming exodus from the real economy are extremely disruptive. Either we will have to rethink completely our notion of what's real, or we will have to accept a drop in economic activity not seen since the 1930s.

Strange though it may seem, the first option is better. Our initial reaction to all of this might be that the events in a synthetic economy are not genuinely real, and therefore can't possibly matter. But many very smart people, from Shakespeare to Baudrillard, have argued that reality is an elastic concept. Society itself, they have said, is best thought of as a kind of virtual reality environment. The cultural world is a construct; you can see evidence for that in the way so many "truths" in "reality" end up being very ephemeral. During the Great Depression, you could buy a sandwich for a dime. It used to be "true" that women were not smart enough to vote. And it was once said in America that bell-bottom pants and tight orange shirts looked good on a man. Many such "truths" have faded away, thankfully. Anthropologist Thomas Malaby has pointed out that virtual worlds and allegedly "real" society share the same structures, the same patterns of behavior. He feels we should refer to virtual worlds not as worlds but as *domains,* merely other places where human behavior plays out.[5] They're all real.

Economic theory supports Malaby's views. The mere fact that the gold pieces in a game are virtual means nothing as far as economic value goes. U.S. dollars are virtual, too; there's no use for them, you can't ride them to work or use them to set a broken bone, yet they have value. The URL microsoft.com is a virtual thing that lives only in the fantasy world of the Internet, yet it clearly has real economic value. So does the URL harvard.edu, even though it is not traded on any market. Trade just reveals what the value is. The important thing is that the value exists.

So far, I've said that there's no difference, either culturally or economically, between production in *Second Life* and production in the real world, meaning that we should pay attention to synthetic world economies as if they were real-world economies. How big is this really, and how big is it likely to get?

As for right now, let's recall how many people are already "virtual worlding": some dozens of millions, with more doing it every day. True, most of them are not in *Second Life* but in fantasy games, games where the object is not to make mansions and hats but to hunt dragons. The economies are roughly the same, however. People make virtual things and sell them to other people in return for virtual money, usually gold pieces. And there are 20 or 30 or 40 million people doing that. Where the people go, goes the economy: big populations mean big economies. Earlier, I said that the amount of real money being spent on virtual currency is in the hundreds of millions of dollars per year. But this trading of dollars for gold is just one type of transaction. Trading gold for magic wands is another. Even though both the gold and the magic wand are virtual, and the trade happens entirely within the virtual world, it still represents an exchange of value. And therefore it counts, in real world terms. The data we have say that virtual-virtual trade is 20 times bigger than virtual-real trade. Since dollars-for-gold-pieces trading adds up to hundreds of millions of real dollars every year, the gold-pieces-for-wands trade must add up to *billions* of real dollars every year. At these levels, the synthetic economy is already equivalent to that of a decent-sized country—Nicaragua, Bahrain, Jamaica, Macedonia.

What about the future? Is there anything to keep people from leaving the real world more or less completely behind? In 2001 I conducted a survey of virtual-world players and found that a shocking 20 percent of them indicated that they think of the virtual world as their true home. The Earth was a place they merely visited from time to time. In Chapter Three, I'll describe how much better virtual worlds will become as the twenty-first century progresses. There's no reason to believe that the desire to escape into fantasy will decrease. On the contrary, as fantasy gets better and better, more and more people will want to spend time in virtual reality.

Will that be technically possible? Sure. It doesn't take much to support a human body at a level sufficient to allow the mind to live synthetically. A room, a bed, a computer, Internet, some food, a toilet. You don't even need an exercise machine. You can already play video games like *Dance Dance Revolution* to keep your body in shape. Once synthetic worlds have physical activity interfaces, "living" in virtual reality won't mean morbid obesity. As a consumer package, all the things you'd actually need are not very expensive when compared to the unnecessary stuff people spend their money on. It is indeed striking to think how much of consumer expenditure in countries like the United States goes to things not necessary to survival. Clear away all those things, and you have the amount of money one would need to earn in a synthetic economy in order to spend all of your time there. Right now, you could earn a wage of $1 to $4 hourly just farming gold from virtual environments and selling it on eBay. Author Julian Dibbell went so far as to test whether one could really make a living selling virtual gold—he could.[6] Yes, people could easily "move" or "migrate" to the virtual world in much the same way that Europeans have migrated to North America. And they will want to. But even a partial migration would matter. Carla only moved 40 percent of her work to the virtual world. When hundreds of millions of people start doing that, it will make a difference for us all.

INTO THE FRONTIER

This exodus puts us back in touch with a phenomenon we thought we had lost forever: the frontier. Virtual worlds are new lands. Several writers have said that the Internet is a kind of new frontier, but we haven't been able to see the specific implications until now.[7] The bottom line is this: When people move from one country to another, both countries change. As synthetic worlds emerge, our real world will return to the situation that America experienced in the first three hundred years of its history. In

1893, historian Frederick Jackson Turner wrote that the closing of the American frontier changed the country forever. The reopening will be just as dramatic. The question is, what will the effects be?

THE EFFECTS OF AN EXODUS

In addition to economic activity, political, social, and cultural activity will migrate as well. Emigrants will develop new ways of being that challenge the ways of the old world. The real world will experience loss, but it will also be challenged to change.

How can we come to grips with these effects? Part II of the book develops some ideas that will help. First of all, it's important to recognize that the one thing virtual worlds provide in abundance is fun, plain and simple. Ask anyone why they play, and they will say "It's fun." So we can predict that the people the real world will lose will be first and foremost those who crave fun. And then we can also predict that the challenges the real world will face will also involve fun. People who spend all their time in a video game will occasionally pop out and ask "Why isn't the real world as fun as my game?" before disappearing again. An understanding of fun will become integral to understanding why the real world is losing people, and what to do about it.

Unfortunately, as I will point out in Chapter Five, we don't understand fun at all. There's no economics of fun and no easy way to build an economics of fun. Economists have found strange things about the nature of human happiness, such as, the money we work so hard to get doesn't make us all that happy. Psychologists have found similar things.[8] Existing research can't quite pinpoint where happiness and fun come from when we are playing a game.

In light of the absence of accepted ideas about fun, Chapter Six sketches out a theory of fun by focusing on the psychological processes that occur during game play. This should help us understand what sorts of people are likely to be lured away by fun synthetic worlds. For better or for worse, though, the answer seems to be "everybody"—because the most sensible theory about fun says that our desire for it is hard-wired and very deep in the brain. Fun-seeking evolved early, not late. Play helps us learn safely how to avoid dangers. For that reason alone, we all love play. That means that if synthetic worlds prove to be basically pretty fun things, every single one of us hairless apes will be attracted to them. True, today there are lots of people who have no interest in the computer and video games of *today*. But games are changing. In 1910, lots of people had no interest in automobiles. Today, everyone has one. You could have predicted that outcome, based on the truth that every hairless ape naturally finds rapid transportation to be incredibly useful, and the prediction that the car industry would eventually figure out how to make cars easy to use. Synthetic worlds are on the same development path: obviously of interest to everybody, and very likely to become an increasingly facile tool. Thus as synthetic worlds expand, the loss to the real world will not be selective and marginal, but rather comprehensive and general.

The pressures that the old world will then face will come from comparisons between the fun to be had in synthetic worlds and the fun to be had in the real world. Chapter Seven considers how virtual-world designers create fun worlds. It treats them as though they are governments, interested only in policies that make people happy. In effect, actually, that's what they are. Because of the competitive pressures of the marketplace, the people who design these huge game worlds do so with the objective of making their users happy all the time. And so they've developed a sort of general fun policy, a series of design norms and strategies that they have learned make most people happy, most of the time.

Chapters Eight and Nine then consider what effects this fun policy will have on the governments of the real world. If future generations grow up socialized in virtual-world environments, they will develop certain expectations about how things are done. When they are then asked to vote on policies in the real world, they will judge those policies in the light of what they have learned. They will expect to see elements of fun policy in the real world. In the end, people will come to see game design and public policy design as basically the same sort of activity. Designing a game for millions of players involves setting a series of rules so that those players will interact in ways that generally leave them feeling happier. Making public policy for a real society involves, again, making rules so that people get along. It's true that the objectives of public policy are generally labeled as "efficiency," "equity," "growth," "justice," and so on, and that the objectives of game design are labeled "fun." But when game players complain about why their games are enjoyable or not, they talk about justice, they talk about equity, they talk about growth, they talk about efficiency. And the underlying objective in the real world for our policies is the improvement of human well-being. Successful game designs improve well-being. It's not much of a stretch to suggest that successful public policies make the real world more fun. If we're looking for handbooks on how to make happy worlds, we need only to look at what the game designers have come up with already.

Chapter Eight explores what a fun economy will look like. Chapter Nine looks at fun society. When real-world governments are asked to make things better, they will increasingly turn to the game designers for advice. The economies and societies we now see in games will eventually become blueprints for the construction of real economies and societies.

WHEN WILL IT HAPPEN?

One answer is that it is already happening. The exodus is already underway. In 2001, perhaps 3 or 4 million people around the globe had some sort of an account in a virtual world. Now, it is in the vicinity of 20 million or 30 million. By the time you read this, it will be 50 percent again as many. Things will continue to move very rapidly. The worlds inside computers are awfully attractive already, and it seems unlikely that anything will happen to make them less attractive. On the contrary, technological improvements and advances in psychosocial entertainment research and development will make synthetic worlds better and better. Current signs suggest that the pace of improvement in virtual worlds will probably be very, very fast. The real world, meanwhile, will puff along as usual. I certainly don't anticipate any major changes that would reduce the ills of contemporary life, no dramatic reduction in congestion and boredom, no dramatic increase in fun and meaning.

Yet as I write this, video games are largely considered toys, and their social impact is being likened mostly to children's television. Politicians like Hillary Clinton and Arnold Schwarzenegger seek to regulate the sale of video games because they feel the violent content they contain is damaging to youth. But games are not toys, and what we do with them can be quite serious.[9] Without getting into the debate about games and violence, I can say that violence is only the tip of the iceberg of social effects. Chapter Ten brings home the breadth of the changes we are about to see, in areas ranging from family structure to our basic understanding of good and evil. Synthetic worlds allow people to form new societies in new lands almost at will. When the American frontier was open, it made space for whole communities built around alternative views of the meaning of human life. Mennonites, Quakers, Amish, and others have made contributions to our culture out of all proportion to their populations, and only because their cultures were both different *and* had a space in which to live. Now that such space is exploding before our eyes and under our virtual feet, we can expect all kinds of new thoughts to emerge. We will be forced to adopt many of the practices of the new cultures being founded on the other side, or the exodus to the virtual will have no end.

CHAPTER TWO

GAME SOCIETIES

What lies behind the claim that so many people will take off to virtual worlds? Basically, it is an awareness that the economic importance of digital fun is growing. The global market for video and computer game hardware and software today stands at about ten billion dollars annually and has risen continuously for the past several years. The term "video game" refers to games played on consoles, whereas "computer games" are played on personal computers. The term "digital game" covers both. Digital games have long been the preserve of the young and nerdy, but that distinction is fading. This is apparently not the sort of thing one gives up as one matures; people born after 1980 seem to continue their gaming with more sophisticated and emotionally involved products. Consistent with this, industry statistics indicate that the average age of video gamers is rising by about one year each year. It is already in the thirties right now. It seems that once people start playing, they don't stop. They may change the kinds of games they are playing, but an interest in interactive entertainment media, once acquired, seems never to fade. The demand for new games is relentless.

The industry that provides digital game entertainment has developed a very large array of different play modes, from single-person exploration games to trivia to multiplayer online poker. The kinds of games that seem to draw people in the most, however, and have the deepest effects on their lives, are massive multiplayer online role-playing games, the *virtual worlds* defined in the previous chapter.

THE GROWING IMPORTANCE OF DIGITAL GAMES

Digital games—*Spacewar* and *Pong*—were invented quickly after the construction of the first networked computers in the 1960s. Why were games such an early application? One has to surmise that fun had something to do with it. If you think about it, in that era it must have been hard to explain to supporters and potential funders how computers worked or what they were for. Anyone who has worked in a large organization or tried to raise money for a business can understand the sales problem: You bring the bigwigs to see your project and all you have to show them is a huge whirring box. Their first question will be "What does this thing do? Show us how it works." And if you're using it primarily to calculate slope coefficients on regression lines, well, that's not going to immediately thrill anybody into writing a check. It has to be explained; you have to walk the group through your computer readouts and discuss the nature of the underlying research and how hard it was to do before you built this huge whirring box. Meanwhile, your visitors just came from the theater, where computerized robots were walking around a space-age apartment, talking to people and cleaning up the trash. Your box just sits there whirring, cranking out reams of meaningless numbers. All in all, that's a tough demo. So you program a little game your visitors can play, something that helps your computer look like at least a distant relative of the ones in the movies. And whether your visitors believe that or not, they still leave the lab on a little high—they got to have a little fun, instead of being pummeled with numbers and bullet points. Digital games solved a real-world problem: putting some fun into dog-and-pony shows.

From this humble start the commercial applications of digital games were quickly recognized, though developing them involved significant booms and busts.[1] Nonetheless, by 1990, game consoles and game-enabled computers were to be found in a very large portion of homes in developed countries, and millions of kids played with handheld game devices. The prevalence of computing technology, some argued, changed the nature of childhood itself.[2]

By the turn of our century, the digital gaming industry had begun to mature into a structure that seems likely to remain stable for some time. Media scholar Dmitri Williams has done the best job of analyzing and reporting the basic structures in the industry.[3] According to his analysis, there are three layers of activity: development, publication, and retail sales. Developers make the games, usually in teams. Some development studios are independent, but others are owned by publishers, and as a result the team sizes vary considerably. A big title might have a development team in the hundreds, while other games have only a few, or even just one, developer. Development involves an incredibly wide range of skills: programming, art, audio, management, and game design. The first four of these can be staffed through established channels; plenty of schools and universities offer degrees in programming, digital art, digital audio, and software development. Game design is a different story; it is a new skill that does not have an established education track. It draws on a very broad set of talents: writing, language, history, psychology, economics, sociology, political science, anthropology, education. Yet none of these fields sees the study of the design of games for fun as one of its core missions. As a result, most stars in game design earn their reputation by making games, rather than by training or pedigree. As will be discussed in Chapter Seven, it is in game development houses, not universities, that the new science of fun is being tested and refined.

Developers complete the games and then turn them over to publishers, who try to sell them. The publishing layer is much more concentrated than the development layers, with giant publishers like Microsoft and Electronic Arts dominating the field. Many of the major publishers are part of even larger global entertainment firms. Publishers exercise considerable sway over the output of the industry; they are the source of advances that allow development houses to work on a game that may not see any sales revenues for many years. Publishers market the title, which increasingly involves relationships with other large players in the entertainment field, such as film companies and toymakers. Tie-ins and licensing have become an important force in determining which games actually get built; bad games derived from a popular movie character will sell, but good games that no one knows about won't. The publisher's interests are driven by a search for the big hits, games that sell millions and millions of copies.

Retailers are the third layer, and their interests are simply in having good products on the shelves. The way games get sold almost certainly has an impact on content. If retailers report that violent or sexy or otherwise flashy box art is what really grabs the passing eyeball, publishers will tell designers to make games that can deliver that kind of content. Games are digital to begin with, so one might think that digital distribution and downloading would be the primary distribution channel. Yet physical distribution remains a dominant retail channel. Major retailers, like Target and Wal-Mart, continue to exert strong influence on what games get sold. Digital downloading seems to predominate only in the area of mobile games—games for phones and handhelds.

With this set up, the industry has successfully created markets for games on all kinds of devices. At any one time, there are several different home game consoles available; games can be played on phones and PDAs; small handheld game consoles can now link to one another for multiplayer use; games persist as a major use of personal computers; and flash games are available all over the web, even in banner advertisements. Cognoscenti in the industry now refer to "ubiquitous gaming": gaming available everywhere, all the time.

All told, hardware and software sales in the digital game industry come to about ten billion dollars annually, which is about the same size as Hollywood's box office revenues. It is also much less than Hollywood's total revenues, which include DVD sales and rentals; and if Hollywood included the sales of DVD players (as the game industry includes the sales of game consoles), the difference would be even greater. Games are not as big as Hollywood, not yet. But they are being played by an extraordinarily wide variety of people, according to the Entertainment Software Association (ESA). Their most recent annual survey indicates that the average age of a gamer is 33; that 25 percent of gamers are over 50; that adult players have on average been playing for 12 years; that there are significantly more women over age 18 playing games than boys under 18. And gaming involves a person more than a film does. My own experience and casual empiricism suggest that a person will watch a film for two hours but play a game for one hundred hours. If a film costs $10 and a game $50, you might expect the game to occupy ten times the number of hours. It is much more than that, however. The social salience of games and their effects seems understated by the size of their market sales.

This growing influence is illustrated by a recent development in the travel industry. Airlines are beginning to allow passengers to play digital games with one another in-flight. Returning from Germany, one of my colleagues reported, "That's the first transatlantic flight that I ever enjoyed, even though seat 19B won most of the time."

If the game industry can make long flights enjoyable, it must be on to something.

WHY DO WE ENJOY DIGITAL GAMES?

Let's introduce some basic reasons why digital games have become an important part of daily life. The fact is, games have had their success in a jungle that already was filled to the brim with other entertainment animals. Some of them are being shoved brusquely to the side as games move forward. Thus whatever games do, they do it better than these displaced forms of entertainment.

One way to think of digital games is as the latest step in a series of media innovations that began transforming the world in the mid-nineteenth century. The sequence runs from photography through radio, film, and TV, and finally to computer and video games. It's worthwhile to pause and reflect on how short that history really is. The scope of human physical development covers millions of years, advanced cultural development some tens of thousands. Here in just 150 years we have invented and deployed a series of tools that allow creators to render whole environments almost as richly detailed and animated as reality itself. Communications scholars Byron Reeves and Clifford Nass of Stanford University determined as much through a lengthy series of studies that tested how the brain reacts to media images.[4] Their finding was that for all practical psychological purposes, media images are initially perceived as real. The reason is simple: the brain evolved in an environment that did not have media in it. Thus when you see a tiger on TV, your brain's first reaction is not "TV tiger" but just "tiger." That reaction dominates only until higher-level brain structures process the tiger and determine that it is not, in fact, in the living room. But the assumption that media images are real is certainly the starting point for all of this processing. Under certain circumstances—a very good movie, for example—we may actually ask the higher structures to let go a bit, to allow us to be in the reality that the media imagery presents us. This drifting off is getting easier and easier, as more recent innovations have made media representations ever more difficult to distinguish from real things.

That's why media are capable of making us excited or sad or flinchy: The brain presumes everything it sees is real, and has to work to remind itself that things on screens are not what they appear to be. Such a protocol makes good evolutionary sense; the brain evolved in the millions of years before media existed, so none of its core structures understand the difference between a real tiger and one on TV. The distinction has to be developed as an abstract pattern of thinking. And making distinctions, according to the work of Annie Lang, an expert on media psychology at Indiana University, takes up some mental resources.[5] Lang's theory holds that the mind has limited resources to allocate to all of its tasks. Of the millions of mental tasks the mind must accomplish in a given split second, the job of reminding itself that the tiger is just a TV tiger is only one. Lang has verified this theory through experiments in which subjects are given tasks to do, and then some other tasks or interventions that can eat up the brain's processing resources. As the theory would predict, these distracting tasks and interventions do slow down the main work the subjects are asked to do.[6] This implies that as media images become increasingly similar to reality, our minds have to do more work to sort out the real from the media.

Lang's theory also says that our minds won't really want to do the work of separating media from reality if the media image is pleasant or motivating at a deep psychological level. Her studies show that media cognition is motivated by core drives that kick in long before we are conscious of them. A heterosexual male's core drives are covert allies in his effort to believe that the picture of the nude woman he is using to masturbate is real. They become his opponent when his neocortex is trying to concentrate on driving and he comes upon a billboard that uses a beautiful female body to advertise beer. I used the example of sex here because it's probably what many readers think of when someone says "core drive" or "inner urge" or "base tendencies." But Lang's motivational system is more than just a catalog of animal urges. The idea is that we have two independent sources of motivation, one "appetitive" (things we like) and one "aversive" (things we don't like). Sex is obviously something we generally like, and so is food; all imagery related to things that a member of homo sapiens might like engages the appetitive system. A tiger or anything that would threaten us, conversely, energizes the aversive system. If we have to fight to get food, both systems get activated to a high level, one pushing, the other pulling. That's exciting. And it's also a main source of media attraction: Media that activate these systems excite us. It seems as though most stories in TV and films are about men and women fighting against something so that they can eventually have sex. How exciting! And given that this is so exciting, the brain keeps telling itself "Don't worry about whether or not this is real—just watch!" In scientific terms, the brain's motivational structures allocate its resources primarily toward ingesting and processing the media's content, rather than judging it as fake and using that information to tone down response from the emotional structure. At a very basic psychological level, we are willing dupes in the media's tomfoolery. And this helps to explain Reeves and Nass' findings that the brain reacts in the same way to media images and real events.

As media, then, games have the same carte blanche with our minds that movies and TV do, yet they can do a whole lot more with it. One obvious feature that games add to the media mix is interactivity. If people get immersed in films, where they do nothing but watch, imagine how much more immersed they must get when they are creating and molding the story. With interactivity, now we have the frontal lobes actively colluding in the project of believing; they are trying to solve some puzzle or talk to some character, which is not only interesting but also eats up still more of the resources that otherwise might go to the job of reminding every other structure in the brain that the whole thing is a construct. This job falls even further into the background due to a number of other features that games and only games have, such as sociality (more on that in a moment), and engagement of other senses, most especially touch (more on that in Chapter Three). Simply put, when a person is immersed in pleasurable game play, the mind has no motivation whatsoever to disbelieve any of the information it is receiving.

Digital games have been succeeding because they offer the mind a congenial entertainment. Their primary competitors for our attention are other media and the real world. Digital games do well relative to other media because they offer much of what those other media do (stories, sounds, images, movement) and some very important things that they do not (interactivity, tactile sensation, sociality). No wonder TV ratings have been falling among people born after 1980.[7] As for the real world, it continues to have the same relative benefits and costs as always.

There's nothing quite like the feeling of holding an infant in your arms. There's also nothing quite like the feeling of his vomit oozing down your chest. A Renaissance faire takes us back to a time so pure and simple that we long to have it again—until we go near the portable toilets, at which point modernity's merits become undeniable. The touch of our lover's hand drives us wild, but her fart grosses us out. Reality remains reality, strongly sensated but unfiltered, raw. It will always command attention, but it has long since abandoned the claim to *all* of our attention. We already live partly in media. Games are just the latest improvement.

ADDING THE SOCIAL INGREDIENT: DIGITAL GAMES AS VIRTUAL WORLDS

Though useful, the view that digital games are just the extension of a long series of media technologies is probably too limiting. If games were just an extension and improvement of TV, I wouldn't bother to write this book. Whatever TV has done to revolutionize daily life, an intensification of it would not cause much more disruption. A TV that is more engaging, more pleasant, more real, would just eat up more of our entertainment time. And perhaps that's what most people think when they hear about the growth of video games: more better entertainment, like TV but more fun. And much of the discussion we hear today has this flavor. For example, games have been attacked because they will supposedly make kids even more fat than TV does; this argument was even the basis for a proposed New York State law in 2003. But let's challenge some of these premises. Are video games played mostly by kids? No. And do video games make you fat, like TV? No. Unlike TV, you have to move when you play video games. And as we will see in Chapter Three, it's not just fingers any more. You have to exercise strenuously in some video games, and in others, the game's tactile stimulations make you move your whole body whether you're thinking about it or not. Digital games are not just an extension of TV, not just another media innovation; they are radically transforming daily life.

I've already argued that games add interactivity, but I think the feature that makes them so transformative, even revolutionary, is the social component they enable. Older forms of media are not consumed collectively, by and large. Yes, people watch movies and TV together, but the presence of other people does not add much of significance to the experience. Occasionally, one joins others in laughing, cheering, or crying, but even here, the dynamics of mental activity remain between the screen and the individual, with other people playing only a background support role. Live sports involve much more interactivity than that—my yelling for a touchdown contributes to a huge volume of sound that I also consume; the collective yelling adds to my enjoyment of the touchdown the Hoosiers eventually score. But does anyone ever say "What I liked about the film was the thrill of crying with all the other people"? Generally speaking, media consumption was an individual affair until online digital games came along.

We can date that event to the mid-1990s, when richly graphical video games first began to enable online play. The core technologies had been invented much earlier, of course. The first digital games in the 1960s involved multiple players connecting through a network. The first game with large groups of players, *MUD*, was invented by undergraduates Richard Bartle and Roy Trubshaw at Essex University in the United Kingdom in 1978. But *MUD* and its descendents were based on textual interactions. In the 1980s, the first graphical multiuser environments were built (Farmer and Morningstar's *Habitat*, and the *Activeworlds* system), but these were not games, properly speaking. The first graphical online world game was *Meridian 59*, developed by the brothers Mike and Steve Sellers and launched in 1996. It made use of the immersive 3D game graphics introduced by John Carmack of id Software. The next launches had 2D graphics: *Ultima Online* by Richard Garriott, launched in 1997, and the Korean game world *Lineage* by NCSoft, launched in 1998. The 3D virtual world *EverQuest* was launched by Sony Online Entertainment in 1999. Collectively, these early worlds amassed more than a million users before the turn of the century. Since then, new 3D virtual worlds have been appearing at about the rate of Moore's Law—doubling every two years or so.

User populations have risen at the same rate, although it is getting harder and harder to measure exactly how many people are playing. In the late 1990s, all games were based on a monthly subscription model. With fees ranging from $10 to $15 monthly, and with account subscriptions given an explicit expiration time (one month, three months, six months, etc.), we could be fairly confident that the total number of subscribers was about the same as the total number of users. At any one time, of course, not all of the accounts would be in use; industry rules of thumb suggest that about 20 to 30 percent of active accounts are present in-world at any one time. But new revenue models have been introduced that break these connections between registrations and use. *Second Life*, for example, offers a free registration to anyone who wants it. You only pay *SL* money if you need land to build something on. On the basis of this system, as of this writing, *SL* has more than five million registered users. However, only about 30,000 people are actually present in the *SL* world system at any one time. Using the industry rule of thumb, this would imply that *SL*'s active account base is only 100,000 to 150,000 accounts (30,000 divided by .30 and .20, respectively). The remaining 4.9 million accounts are people who signed up to take a look and then left— since there's no sunset on a free registration, all of these visitors continue to count in *SL*'s registration base, more or less forever. We might then develop a new rule of thumb, that free registration world populations compare to subscription worlds at a 90 percent discount. That would mean, for example, that it takes ten *Second Life* free subscriptions to equal one *World of Warcraft* paid subscription. But then what do we make of a world like *Habbo Hotel,* that claims over 50 million registered characters? According to the game's website, www.habbo.com, only 7,589 users are actually present this Sunday evening, usually the busiest across the industry. Using the role-playing game usage metric, these 8,000 current users would be equivalent to about 30,000 active game accounts. The implied discount to *Habbo*'s population is a number with a lot of zeros (30,000 ÷ 50 million, or 0.0006), meaning you need 1,700 *Habbo* registrations to get the use equivalent of one *World of Warcraft* registration. The only point here is that *Habbo*'s actual contribution, though clearly substantial, is open to debate, and muddles any effort to get a firm sense of how important this phenomenon is and how rapidly it is growing.

If all virtual worlds simply published an accurate count of current usage, we could tally those across worlds and across time to come to a decent estimate. But actually very few worlds are as upfront about usage as *Second Life* and *Habbo* are, and thus we are largely in the dark. The best bet is to pay the most attention to paid-subscription game registrations, since these have a price attached and can expire. This adds up to 15 million or so, every one of them someone who is engaged enough in the game world to be paying a substantial amount of money every month. And to this total we should add several million for all of the worlds that have free registrations. In other words, while total registrations to virtual worlds are probably well over 100 million, a conservative total estimate of actual users would be 20 million; 30 million is probably more accurate. Whatever the number, it is dramatic growth. Ten years ago, a few worlds with several hundred thousand actual users; today, dozens of worlds with 20 or 30 million actual users

However we count their size, there is no question that when virtual worlds appeared they offered something very much unlike what digital games had offered before. They were persistent, visually engaging, and emotionally engaging as a result of the depth of game play. Moreover, these places were truly worlds in terms of their size. Each was capable of supporting thousands of players at the same time, enough to allow the emergence of genuine social forces: markets, power hierarchies, reputation systems, language innovations, prestige. Early observers recorded the emergence of these ordinary human structures with a mix of amusement and shock. In 2001, Elizabeth Kolbert found stories of avatars stripping themselves naked and puking in protest of some change in game rules worthy of a piece in *The New Yorker*. There really is nothing shocking about it, though—analytical social science has been able to pare down most core social structures to their base behavioral elements, and it turns out that those behaviors do not depend on the arena in which humans interact. It doesn't matter that people are interacting in a video game; what matters is that they are people, and they are interacting. All of human sociality follows.

Thus digital games, once online, immediately became hosts to genuine societies. This is why a term like *synthetic worlds* makes sense. These online game worlds are built to look very much like the real world, with trees and oceans and mountains, food and water, and creatures wandering around. They persist just like the real world does. And one encounters other real people in them, people whom you meet as often as you meet your neighbor (indeed more often, given the isolation that characterizes the real world today). Online games are very much like our world, except that they are built, crafted, like a copy or model. Hence, *synthetic world*s. Synthetic worlds thus are a subset of digital games, combining the techniques of game design with the technology of networked graphical sociality.

As I write this, synthetic worlds are the most dynamic and energetic part of the entire digital games sector. According to the Entertainment Software Association, 19 percent of frequent gamers said they played online games in 2000; by 2006, the percentage had risen to 44 percent. Single-player gaming remains as fun as always, but it is not being treated as the future of the industry. Rather, recent developments suggest that *all games are going to go online* within a very few years. And when they do, they will all acquire a societal dimension.

Sociality makes a huge difference in the impact of games. Now you are not only interacting with a system, you are interacting with others through that system. Sometimes that involves competing with them over resources the system provides, using tools that the system also provides. Other times it involves allying with other people to defeat a challenge that the system provides to all of you. Or, you ally with others to defeat other alliances. Or your alliance can join with other alliances, making a super-alliance. The game systems allow human-to-human interactivity comparable to that of the real world.

When games get social, the brain suddenly must devote resources to all of its social structures in addition to calculation, perception, memory, and so on, leaving still less room for reality assessment. If games in general make it hard for the brain to disbelieve virtuality, social games make it even harder. Many social structures involve deep pleasure, and hence would strongly motivate the brain to allocate resources to them. It is well known that people make friends and consummate romantic relationships online. Humans are also known to stimulate themselves with pornographic images, and to have sex over the phone. In an online game today, it is possible for two players to construct a pornographic image for themselves by creating a handsome character and stripping it naked. Two people can do this and show their naked bodies to each other. They could then add movement to the characters using simple system commands that most games provide—/dance, /kiss, /hug, /kneel, /sleep. Finally, they could use Internet telephony which is now a common communication system between game players, to flesh out their scene with their voices. Such a scene would engage quite a bit of the brain's resources (not to mention the body's), leaving very little for the brain's reality-check mechanism. And since cognition is motivated, according to Lang, the reality-check mechanism would only succeed if it somehow convinced the allocation structure that giving it resources would be good for the brain's owner—would help him get something he wants or avoid some threat. Given the scenario depicted, a reality check is probably not something a person would want at this particular moment. Indeed, reality would be perceived as a threat. The social dimension, here exemplified bluntly by sexual play, adds immensely to the immersive quality of the environment.

And sociality I would argue is what makes digital games a transformative technology as well. The big difference here is not that people feel very immersed, it is that they feel immersed *together*. The situation is not that some individuals have gone off to their rooms to read a book or play a game. Rather, crowds of people are ducking out collectively. And they are conscious of that collectivity. Gamers refer to themselves as members of a given server of a given game: "Hey everybody, I'm Gilbi from *Everquest* Bristlebane—how are you?" Media and games expert T. L. Taylor spent many hours within a particular gamer community and came away impressed with the cohesion and persistence of that community.[8] A gamer comes to feel that there is not just a new world sitting inside the computer, but a new country as well. The prospect of a new community, society, or even state rapidly emerging on its own territory ought to give us pause.

This emerging civitas in virtual worlds could be seen as the gradual realization of the independence of the Internet. In the early days of the net, John Perry Barlow offered a declaration of independence of cyberspace, and in the early days of synthetic worlds, Raph Koster offered a declaration of the rights of avatars. When these documents were crafted, there really was no political entity for them to refer to; the Internet, and virtual worlds, were small. By contrast, the American Declaration of Independence was proclaimed by a Congress of representatives of 13 prosperous states with millions of citizens and well-established military forces. The French Declaration of the Rights of Man was proclaimed by a National Assembly with an awareness of decades if not centuries of inherited right to comment on public matters, and a newfound sense of its own economic power. In comparison, the Internet declarations were made when the population of cyberspace had self-awareness, but no political authority or economic clout. Given that, there is no reason at all to expect that mere declarations would be enough to make the Internet its own jurisdiction. On the contrary, however, as eminent legal scholar Larry Lessig has argued, the islands of autonomy once present on the Internet are being relentlessly hunted down and eradicated, sometimes for the good of the world, but often merely in the service of economically worthless but politically powerful cabals like the music distribution industry.[9] Sovereignty follows economic and political power, not vice versa. The country to which Barlow and Koster referred was not at that time economically powerful or even politically self-conscious. It was populated by some tens of thousands of Internet experts whose salaries came largely from real-world companies. The Internet arena in which these early users lived was primarily a land of asynchronous text messages where little of value persisted. Internet communities, such as they were, did not have an economic or political or cultural base required for a civitas. The cart was before the horse.

But now the horse has caught up. Virtual worlds today unquestionably have significant economic, political, and cultural resources. They still have nowhere near what they would need to become independent states, and I am not about to argue that they should become independent states. The legal dependence or independence of virtual-world communities will be determined by the way we respond to the economic, political, and cultural clout that these communities will come to possess. Today, the economic clout is not at a level that would allow a virtual world to impose trade sanctions against the real world, for example, but it is at a level that allows users to feel economically invested in the place, and to draw a substantial income from it. The economies of virtual worlds produce a substantial stream of production and consumption goods, only a fraction of which become liquidated into real money. These sources of economic power will grow. Economically speaking, there is a *there* there, and it is getting bigger.

Similarly, there is growing political and cultural substance in virtual worlds as well. You see the politics when game developers—the local government, for all intents and purposes—alter the game's design in response to the concerns of the community. This happens all the time, most often in response to a rabid horizontal equity claim. It can be observed on the game's forums in streams of proclamations like "Nerf wizards now or I am canceling my account!1!eleven!!," a proclamation whose heat and anger is evident even if the actual point requires much translation (which I will do in a moment). These political drives can be quite effective and invoke rich symbolism as well. Once while visiting a company I shall not name, a very prestigious designer received a manila envelope mailed by a fan that contained something bulky and perhaps interesting. He decided to open it and see. Dumping the contents on his desk, we found a set of the CDs for his game, each one cut precisely in half. No note attached, but the message was clear: "The policy change you just enacted stinks." If enough people do it, such political tactics work.

We can see growing cultural substance in the form of a unique synthetic world's language. A wide range of cultural values and symbols are being rendered into reality alongside the fantasy money that gets all the attention. Terms like *nerf* ("to weaken") and practices like using numbers to replace letters and punctuation (using *1* in place of the exclamation point) demonstrate the emergence of a new dialect. The language then turns on itself, distancing it further from real-world language use. The word *eleven* above stands for "11," which was standing in for "!!." In the same vein, the name *Afive$g0bl!n* really means "Assgoblin." The point of the strange spelling is to avoid automatic name-checkers, programs sent out by game companies to prevent players from calling themselves things like Assgoblin.[10] Obviously, they do it anyway. Perhaps just because. And therefore what we have is a conflict over language, to which the virtual-world residents respond by inventing their own.

All of this economic, political, and cultural power has emerged within virtual worlds; it did not emerge in e-mail or chat communities. One reason is sheer size: No chat community has millions of members, yet there are literally millions of people concerned about the upcoming change to the rogue class in *World of Warcraft*. Almost all of those people speak with some fondness of the rogues they knew in *Ultima Online* or *Lineage* or some other gateway game. Hundreds of thousands compare *Warcraft's* rogues to the swashbucklers in *EverQuest II*. Meanwhile, users of *EVE Online*, the space game, or *Second Life*, the non-game world, having no rogues per se, wave their hands over these concerns. Yet they are conversant with them. They understand what a nerf is, and what a buff is (the opposite of a nerf). They understand the difference between a "stun" and a "root" (one keeps a player from doing anything, the other only keeps him from moving). They understand the following policy declaration: "Improved Sprint: The Sprint Ability now has a 50 percent chance to break all movement-impairing effects." (Translation: The rogue class is going to be buffed in that rogues who use their sprint ability also have a chance to get out of stuns and roots.) The number of people who understand and care about such things has grown quite large, and their concerns are solidified by collective awareness, cultural distinctiveness, and economic resources.

And this is where it gets strange for the rest of us. Our first reaction might be that we do not care what happens to the "sprint ability." Why should we? This is just a rule in somebody's silly game. But when the game is being played by tens of millions of people who are all jointly conscious of their communal interest in the outcome, the rule they are concerned about is not so silly any more. Overlooking the concerns of tens of millions of people is a mistake that governments make only at their peril, as the long history of toppled dictators makes clear. Political philosophers such as Robert Dahl defend democratic governance because, at the very least, its structures are designed to actively solicit the interests of the people.[11] It may not act on them immediately or fairly, but at least the government will know. Economic philosophers in the Austrian school, such as Ludwig von Mises and Friederich von Hayek, correctly predicted that communism would have trouble simply on the basis of information problems. These "information economists" argued that the most important thing a free market system does is allow prices to move freely. Prices then reveal where resources are most valued. That kind of information is tough to get, which is why communist countries always had too many rubber boots and not enough toilet paper. Gathering up and getting to know the desires of *all* the people is critical to the success of any civic order. And here we have tens of millions of people spending countless millions of hours in these games, where they quite unabashedly care a lot about the sprint ability of rogues. At some point, at some level of virtual-world population, economic prowess, and cultural self-awareness, the sprint ability of rogues becomes a legitimate policy issue for us all.

Or not. We may steadfastly insist that it does not matter. Even if one hundred million Americans are spending 80 hours a week in a given virtual world, the policies and events of that world will *still* not matter to us, we might say. Very well; but to close out a set of concerns from our own policy arena is to effectively cede jurisdiction over them to others. It is not clear at this point who exactly would pick this jurisdiction up. If it is the players themselves, then perhaps it might be time for some kind of grand declaration of sovereignty.

But regardless of who has jurisdiction over the events in a virtual world, the fact is that lots of people will collectively care about them. In that sense alone, the design structure of virtual worlds will have significance. Anything that hundreds of millions of people care about is an important thing. Its importance becomes unavoidable, not because we have been persuaded that it matters, but because so many others have been— we have trouble talking to them about anything else. *We will have lost their attention.* In the information age, that's the same as losing them completely.

All of this stems from the communal, civic, and social nature that digital games acquired when they morphed into shared, persistent, Earth-like environments. When they became virtual worlds, digital games added the verifications of society to the fantasies they were creating. The gold coins that single-player games had always had became currencies that traded against the dollar. The rules that single-players games had always had now became political footballs. The strange lores and languages that had always been found in single-player games now became genuine aspects of shared human cultures. Previous online groups have not had the money, the rulesets, and the lore that games have, and so they had no hope of really mattering to the rest of us. They may have had a persistent community, but that community's interests and resources were still drawn largely from the real world. Once games came online, online communities suddenly had interests and resources that were only online. The primary use of gold pieces is not to buy dollars, but to buy magic wands and potions. The center of social gravity in a chat community remains offline, but the center of social gravity in a virtual world is completely online. That's where the things people care about actually live. The discussion is most about things inside the worlds, not outside them. Most important, the user's attention is almost completely immersed in the events of that world, not the real world.

And that constant drain of attention, which may be persistent and widespread in coming decades, is the force that may induce a fun revolution in the real world. Because what are these worlds about except fun? They are designed primarily as games, and even when they are not (as with *Second Life*), the presumption is that no one will spend time in these environments if they are not fun. A virtual world's entire existence is predicated on the provision of good experiences for the user. It has to be better than reality.

Now, often a virtual world will be better than reality in ways that reality cannot replicate. For example, you can flap your arms and fly in a virtual world, but not in the real world. At the same time, reality will always provide things that virtual worlds cannot, such as the pleasure of eating flourless chocolate cake. But there are plenty of things that can be provided by both virtual worlds and the real world; their competences overlap significantly. The overlap is obviously not at the physical level, it is at the social level. In terms of social order, the real world and the virtual world have the same tools and the same objectives. The tools are things like wage rates, job opportunities, education systems, and taxes. The objectives are to provide a set of institutions that allow the governors to retain the support of the people (and thus keep their jobs). From this standpoint, there is no reason why a virtual world's governors could not come to a better solution than those of the real world. It is possible that a virtual world could provide a civic, social, economic, and political order that is superior to that of the real world.

For now, it is sufficient to say that virtual worlds are societies where fun matters. The designers of virtual worlds have made a grab for attention, much like a military foe might try to grab territory, and the weapon they have developed, the mechanism of play, is powerful and well-suited to the task.

CHAPTER THREE

WORLDS OF
THE FUTURE

What are the chances that technologies and game systems will become *less* fun over the next 50 years? It seems highly unlikely. Here's a series of tests I've given myself. Think of the best movie you've seen recently. Focus on the environments, the breathtaking mountains, the huge battles, the heaving oceans, the charming villages. Most likely, they were created by some sort of computer graphics engine. If the movie was made in the year 2002, that level of graphics capability was present in your desktop in 2005 (actually much sooner, but let's be conservative). That means your game character could explore environments like the ones in the movie. Next, think about the most recent animated movie you've seen. Whatever level of sophistication and realism you're seeing in the movie, you will have on your computer screen in a couple of years. Finally, think of the best movie you've ever seen. Think of the story and the acting. Eventually, video games will have stories like that. And if we let the horizon stretch out far enough, artificial intelligence agents—robots that control the nonplayer characters in the video game world—will become excellent actors. Sure, they are completely cheesy right now, but soon we can expect acting at a community-theater level, then at a grade-B film level—still quite melodramatic, but fun—and finally good enough to be cast in the glorious dramatic narrative that your own playing will always be. The bottom line is that eventually you're going to be able to immerse yourself in environments that are as entertaining as your favorite movie. Video games really are the predecessors of future holodeck-like tools. Some aspects of that will come quickly, others will take time. But it will happen. How can we be so sure? Well, it becomes fairly obvious when you realize that advances in computing technology seem unlikely to slow down, and we don't need much more technology to deliver truly stunning experiences.

We are already seeing in video game graphic design a retreat from realism. The machines have the capability to render a medieval fantasy world very nearly photo-realistically, but nobody wants to see acne. And when scientists invent smell engines, you can bet that the smells of open sewage and unwashed bodies are unlikely to be replicated, realistic or no. So not every technological advance will matter. Rather, the two areas of technology that will be most significant are raw computer power, which enables more things to be done, and game systems, which will increase our enjoyment.

Truly, in this space advances come almost more quickly than a person can predict and record them. But among the changes that are obviously coming, there are a few that will have deep implications.

ALL GAMES ONLINE

The first thing one recognizes on the immediate horizon is that every game is acquiring some kind of persistent online component. We are currently in the midst of a transition to a new set of video game console hardware. The main players in this fight are Microsoft's Xbox 360, Sony's Playstation III, and Nintendo's Wii. In the wars of expectation management, the online capabilities of the competing systems have been given prominence. Connecting consoles through the Internet enables a number of enhancements to game-play that having nothing to do with game design itself—such as quick downloads of patches, instant messaging with other players, the formation of ad hoc local-area network parties, and so on. But our main interest here, obviously, is that these systems will enable the virtual-world model, which until now has been primarily written to personal computer protocols. PC games make up a comparatively small fraction of the overall markets. When consoles connect to the network, we can expect virtual worlds to expand into that environment and occupy a much greater share of all gaming than they do now.

Consider the large population of sports games enthusiasts. Sports games are a big fraction of console game sales. Students tell me of nights spent betting on a goofy racing game, $20 (or a shot) per race. The sports network ESPN has broadcast competitions in which real football players compete on console football games. This is clearly multiplayer play, though only at the level of two to four players. But the potential for massively multiplayer sports games is fairly clear.

It thus seems reasonable to predict that every game will eventually go online in some fashion. That doesn't mean that every player will always play multiplayer games, though. When a game goes online, it does not necessarily become an environment where everyone constantly plays with others. Indeed, researchers have combed through reams of data from virtual worlds and determined that a large fraction of play time is spent "solo," that is, not formally connected to other players in a group.[1]

That means the player may occasionally stop to chat with someone, or group up for short periods of time to accomplish a limited objective. All the while, they may be speaking to other members of their "guild," a larger organization of 50 to 200 players that serves social and organizational purposes but does not directly play together. But within this context, the player is often just freely following her own desires and objectives. This seems to work very well from a game design perspective: The player playing alone gets to feel all the thrills of a single-player game—being independent, self-reliant, effective, powerful—and also have all of these feelings validated by the presence of other people in the environment. You can rescue the princess alone in a single-player game as well as in a multiplayer one, but in the multiplayer context, you get applause from other real people. Single-player play is better when embedded in a multiplayer context. Thus even single-player games are likely to eventually have some kind of online component added to them, whether that be a player-matching service or a virtual world. For every game, the Internet will play a role in shaping a community of interest.

ACCESS EVERYWHERE

All of these online games will be accessible from anywhere. Cell phones can now be used to access the Internet anywhere. Wireless networks sprout and extend their range. Bluetooth technology components are starting to appear on heads and hands. This will eventually mean eyepieces that show screens and rings that send hand-motion commands.

Game devices are participating in all of this. The Nintendo DS handheld game machine allows two users to link up wirelessly; there's no turning back for pocket-sized consoles. The emergence of the mobile game industry presages a future in which all personal communication devices enable quick access to games, which will be, of course, online. Since game applications tend to lead every new technology, it is likely that the first heavy users of Bluetooth personal screen and tiny controller capabilities will be gamers.

Games will be available to every person, all the time. The industry refers to this as "ubiquitous gaming" and treats it as fait accompli. I would only add "online" to the phenomenon, since I think, based partly on what I see in airports and cars these days, that people jumping into games on the go will do so to connect to other people rather than just play solitaire.

AVATARS AND DRESS UP

Now let's discuss what's going on *inside* the games, in game design. That too is going to get better.

Let's return to the sports game example. When people play sports games on consoles, there is clearly a strong but unexploited role-playing component. The fellow from Rockford who always dreamed of playing quarterback for the Bears undoubtedly chooses the Bears as his game team for that reason. Then, his passes are completed into the end zone of a faithfully reconstructed Soldier Field. All this situation needs is persistence, scope, and depth in the design of the game world, and it can become a powerfully motivating virtual world. Our friend from Rockford might now play quarterback on a team of fellow Bears fans, some of whom play linebacker, running back, and defensive end. Evidence from fantasy games suggests that some players will even enjoy the less glamorous spots, like placekicker. The evidence is the ongoing popularity of "healing" classes, players whose job is primarily to keep other players alive as they fight monsters. Some players, myself included, really enjoy this kind of support role. Bashing monsters is not so fun to me; choosing who lives or dies is. Similarly, some players will care not about scoring touchdowns, but rather about being an important part of a team with the potential of winning the big game with a single kick. Game designs tend to reward this diversity of interests.

I know from personal experience that the job of healing a group of five to ten other players has been made into an incredibly challenging and engaging task. It is triage, in effect, except that the group is still under attack, and letting the wrong fellow die means that everyone dies. The design plays to that importance, giving healers the ability to observe the hitpoints of all the players and a wide varieties of cures and heals to address any given situation. *World of Warcraft* offers healers an ability called "Spirit of Redemption" that works like this: When the healer is himself killed, he is instantly brought back as a redeemer spirit for a period of ten seconds. During those ten seconds, he is impervious to all pain, damage, and enemy spells. He can cast whatever spells he has. A healer's job involves knowing what to do with those ten seconds of grace. Similarly, a placekicker or offensive lineman in a football virtual world can be given action systems that are engaging and interesting, mastery of which can really make a difference in the team's success. The world could be given an engaging lore and a rich social background, so that players have an arena in which to show trophies of their successes. Potential deep-immersion users of this kind of sports virtual world include just about every person who is a fan of real-world sports. That's a large population.

In general, I would predict that almost every gaming system will acquire some kind of 2D or 3D avatar implementation in a persistent environment. The environment may not be a richly backstoried world, but it will be a permanent place in which the avatar can at least stand and per-

WORLDS OF THE FUTURE

form a few actions. The avatar will be changeable: Clothes, hair, and gear will be modifiable by the user. Those items will be alienable, that is, the user can take them off of their own avatar and give them to another user. It follows directly from this that there will be an economy in these items, and with that economy, a virtual currency. If the game's owners do not implement a trading mechanism, players will use eBay or some other online market. If the game's owners do not implement a currency, one will emerge: the item that is most convenient to use (stackable in large quantities, weightless, rare, stable-valued).

The move to online goes hand in hand with the fullest possible expression of self in the online environment: at this time, the avatar. Everything we've learned about games and online environments says that people have an almost irrepressible desire to construct little models of people and places and display them as an extension of their own being. Every successful virtual world allows a wide variety of avatar looks and millions of variations on dress. And with dress goes the game of reputational hierarchy: Who is dressed up the best? In the real world, people will spend incredible amounts of money to get a car that does exactly the same thing as another car, but just looks cooler. We can say the same thing about houses and clothes. These same preferences mean that a game company would miss a gold mine if it failed to allow people to dress up their avatars in alienable items whose production the company could control. This is true regardless of the application. It could be a role-playing game, or a football game, or a casual card game. Is it possible to imagine a virtual Vegas that did not have cowboys, swingers, sheiks, divas, and showgirls? Thus we can reliably predict that games that go online will also go avatar, picking up the full systems of gear, trade, and virtual currency. A rich level of sociality and deeper immersion will follow. In the future, playing any game at all will involve some kind of virtual-world experience.

TOUCH

If all of the predictions made so far come true, everyone in the world who has a computer will also have ubiquitous persistent access to a wide variety of virtual worlds. These worlds will contain fun games to play as well as opportunities to build characters that have a certain look. Soon, those characters will touch one another, and the players who control them will feel those touches.

One senses that touch is a desired feature by the way players treat their avatars already. In many worlds, players can only craft their look from a fairly tightly controlled (though extensive) menu of choices, but in others, players make themselves look however they wish. Early evidence from user-content worlds like *Second Life* and *The Sims Online* suggests that when users have complete freedom to build their avatars and their homes, they often build erotic playboys and girls and embed them in fetish playgrounds. Literally. Media researchers Jeffrey and Shaowen Bardzell spent several months exploring the fetish communities that have become emergent in *Second Life,* reporting a fascinating level of attention to detail when it comes to sex gear, fetish clothing, dungeons, and avatar positions and acts.[2] In worlds where users do not have that much control over content, they find workarounds. "Naked mods" are common. "Mod" is gamer lingo for a modification of game software that a user can overlay on the game from his own computer. Mods are easy to use; you just download a file to your computer, click the icon, and the mod is automatically installed onto your game. The mod works by taking the information that the game sends to your screen and altering it; for example, when the game tries to draws a maple tree on your screen, a mod could take that instruction and replace the maple tree with a pine tree instead. In the case of the naked mod for *World of Warcraft*, the mod replaces the default nude avatars, which designers have prudently given underwear, with avatars who are truly nude. As one mod author described his program, the mod gives avatars "full nudity, complete with hair and nipples." The game makers can do nothing about this; the mod program is acting on files already in the user's computer, with the user's permission.

Perhaps it goes without saying, but a major driving force in the development of games is the crafting of fully satisfying sexual experiences. On the other hand, it needs to be said because much of this drive is quite clearly left unspoken on both the supply and demand side. Male gamers did not publicly clamor for better breast action, and game companies did not publicly proclaim an R&D investment in improving breast physics, yet those physics have observably improved since 2003.[3] This remarkably quiet development suggests that many players are interested in better sexual content in games, but none of them wants to be exposed as a horny devil. Meanwhile, game makers do not want to be perceived as pornographers. Building games that are amenable to naked mods is one solution: The developers can credibly claim to have kept things alluring but modest, while the players can get the nudity they want.

There is also evidence that the drive to improve sexual content will have a dramatic effect on the quality of games in general. The issue here is one of interface. We already have force-feedback in handheld game controls (the controller vibrates when a bomb goes off). Recently, vibrating gamer recliners with embedded subwoofers have come on the market. The application of vibrating implements to sexual gaming should be obvious to everyone. In an article appearing a very long time ago in Internet years (2002), game writer Jane Pinckard described her experience with the "Trance Vibrator" that came along with the console game *Rez*.[4] There were no instructions, but she related that it was pleasurable to relax with this implement while her boyfriend played the game. In a 2005 follow-up, Pinckard reported that an enterprising user had modified an Xbox game console to support a genuine sex-toy vibrator.[5] Meanwhile, the sex toy industry is moving forward on its own; in 2004, a *Wired News* correspondent reported on the Sinulator, a worn device that can be remotely controlled by another person over the Internet.[6] There is clearly a convergence point to all of this, and it involves sex play using advanced touching interfaces.

There are already several sex-themed virtual worlds in the works, and if the explosive growth in Internet pornography is any indication (400 percent growth in six years, according to one report), they will not only succeed but also drive investment in improved touch interfaces.[7] Improvements in touch will do more than improve online game sexual content (for better or worse); they will improve all gaming. Sexual haptics are not just about the pelvis; the demands of sensitive sexual touching will lead to more precise hand controls that are of interest in a wide variety of contexts.

At the other end of the spectrum from sensitive touching we find gross motor activities like jumping and running. Interface devices that rely on gross motor skills have already been released, such as dance mats for the console game *Dance Dance Revolution*. Game attachments to treadmills and exercise bikes are a natural adaptation. The Sony Eyetoy, released in 2003, is a camera that watches you and then translates your body movements into game controls. The Nintendo Wii controller is designed to be waved around; better get up off the couch if you want to win the bowling match. There is every indication that gaming will not remain a sedentary activity for long, as touch controls extend to more parts of the body with more and more refinement.

EMOTIVE AI

Advances in the credibility of game characters are sprouting up in many places. Online Alchemy, a just-under-the-radar group run by one of the early virtual-world creators, Mike Sellers, has designed and trademarked a "people engine" for creating believable artificial people for virtual environments. At the University of Southern California's Institute for Creative Technologies (ICT), a group of researchers under the leadership of Professor Jonathan Gratch has been working on interactive emotions systems for computational models. It is part of the ICT's "virtual humans" project, which aims to create more realistic artificial intelligence agents for interactive software. A main supporter of these efforts is the U.S. Department of Defense, which hopes to greatly reduce the cost and improve the value of training for soldiers who may face emotionally intense situations. Other groups are also working on improving the way that artificial intelligence handles emotions.

The possibility for game applications is fairly clear: As immersive as the games are already, just wait until the various nonplayer character (NPC) wizards and orcs acquire something like real personalities. Past work by the Affective Computing Group at MIT indicates that it does not take much for a computer to touch a human being on an emotional level. Current projects involve how to capture a person's emotional state and use it in programs. This research and the work at ICT both point toward future games with a very deep level of emotional sophistication.

INTEGRATED COMMUNICATIONS

In most virtual worlds, players can instantly send small text messages to one another. In some, like *Second Life* and *EverQuest,* players can also send instant messages to other players outside the world. Most games have an in-world mail functionality. Most have discussion forums, either inside the world or outside. *Second Life* allows users to browse the web from within the world, as well. They can also watch movies and TV. While only a few games come with a voice communication protocol explicitly, users who want that kind of communication can easily set it up. Companies like Teamspeak and Ventrilo have implemented voice-over-Internet systems that a gamer group can obtain and use quickly. Meanwhile, phones and other handheld devices will become input devices that enable access to the game world at all times.

All of this points in the direction of completely integrated communications systems. And this is another surprising thing about virtual worlds: They look like video games, but in fact they are the most advanced form of communications systems. They are body based, like the first real-world communication system, and they handle a digitized input rather than an analog one. That is to say, the avatar is a crude digital rendering of the human body and handles body-to-body communications about as well as the first digital photo systems handled pictures: slowly, with a pretty high granularity. But that will improve. The synthetic world *there* has avatars who can look bored, shrug, slump, or make eyes at you. The range of bodily communications available seems to rise continuously. Add to this the increasing integration of web, voice, email, and chat, and you can see that virtual worlds are becoming a one-stop communications solution. Anyone who chooses to put their attention in a virtual world will not face any penalty of being cut off from real-world communications. Rather, integrated communications can only make the worlds more fun.

COMPREHENSIVE CULTURAL AND
LITERARY OFFERINGS

In recent history, writers have shown themselves to be adept at creating entire fantasy worlds in which to set their stories. Perhaps J. R. R. Tolkien's Middle Earth is the most successful of these; it seems that Middle Earth has been imitated countless times, in that most of the early virtual worlds have involved medieval fantasy and there are always dwarves and gnomes and elves running around in these places. But anyone can call to mind a lengthy list of fantasy realms that it would be fun to visit. The world of Star Wars has had an implementation, in *Star Wars Galaxy*. There is a *Matrix Online*. A *Star Trek Online* is supposedly in development.

Meanwhile, in the game industry as a whole most publishers feel that having a good license is an easy way to make a game profitable. These days, it is rare that a blockbuster movie appears without a game associated with it. A quick route to large sales figures is to license the rights to a popular cultural icon—Spider-Man, say—and make a game about him. Pre-existing stories and characters are known to be very helpful in giving a game a good chance at success.

Of course, the catalog of "pre-existing stories and characters" from which the industry might draw is massive: Every story that has ever been written could conceivably be implemented as a game. Much as the film industry spent a tremendous amount of the previous century rendering good old stories in the new medium, game designers may spend much of the twenty-first century doing the same for games. In doing so, they will be satisfying the longing that we have all had for a book or a film or a play not to end. There is something about the atmosphere of a tale that has its own distinct fascination, and virtual worlds replicate atmosphere.

Now think of every literary, cinematic, dramatic, or historical atmosphere you've ever yearned to be immersed in. I predict that the game industry will eventually make virtual worlds to capture that atmosphere, in the same way that the film industry has made motion picture versions of every good tale that's been written (and many not-so-good ones). Those who yearn for Dickens' London will walk its cobbled streets. Heathcliff will await discovery in Wuthering Heights. Ancient ceremonies will be practiced at Stonehenge. Shakespeare's King Richard III will be cut down at Bosworth Field. And that's just in England! Travel west with the pioneers, build the Great Wall, live the Arabian Nights, witness the transfiguration of the Lord.

In short, the cultural and literary breadth and depth of games can only expand. As they do, more and more people will discover some environment that seems to have been crafted just for them, just to suit their deepest longings. The desire to be "in there" as opposed to "out here" will strengthen.

USER CONTENT

In game design today, any constraints on the user must be justified in terms of pleasurable challenge or technical feasibility. For example, one reason you often cannot break windows in games is because the processors cannot handle the on-the-fly execution required of thousands of shards of glass flying all over the place. There are exceptions; for example, the designers think it would be fun to have the user jump through this one window and fall onto the melon cart below. But you can't have every window breakable, because that would create a tremendous computing problem. It might also present a design problem as well. The user needs to feel free all the time, unless some constraint makes the world more fun. Constraints are of course essential to the design of games; the user needs to face challenges and puzzles in order to feel the satisfaction of advancing through them. If you allow players to do absolutely everything they can think of, it becomes hard to construct effective challenges. If all windows break, then the character might jump through the other window and land not on a melon cart (which then leads to a pleasant interaction with the fruit-seller), but on a donkey that quickly carries him off to a boring part of the scenery. Balancing user agency with problem satisfaction is a difficult task.

Indeed, creating content is generally difficult. Since 2004 the cost of game design has been rising far more rapidly than sales.[8] The reason costs are rising is that game design is a labor-intensive business. Solving those problems of melon carts, donkeys, and windows requires a refined intuition about what's fun and what's not fun.

One obvious solution to the problems of labor and cost is user-created content. We've already seen that users are more than happy to modify games to suit their own purposes. It makes sense to have them do it, since they are the best judges of whether a constraint is too easy or too hard. Thus it might seem that the ultimate point of convergence here is to have users build their own games completely. It completely respects user agency, and solves the game design cost problem.

That is indeed the premise and business model of *Second Life*. *SL* is not a game, it is an environment in which users can build anything they want. *SL*'s owners hope that at least some users will build content that is entertaining for other users. To encourage good production, *SL* allows users to make money off of the things they create. The gambit is that a small cadre of very talented users will make content so good that a large number of ordinary users will come into *SL* to see it. The ordinary users would then pay the content creators for the content, and the content creators would pay *Second Life* for the land.

With such a business model, *Second Life* is freed from the content creation crunch. And it fully respects the agency of all of its users. The open question at this writing is whether enough good content will be created. It certainly seems likely that if one could harness the creative energy of all the millions and millions of people out there, something special would have to come out of it eventually.

At the other end of the spectrum, we have the huge role-playing worlds like *EverQuest* and *World of Warcraft*. Here there is much less user content creation than in *SL*. Still, users can put together content in unique ways (by wearing different clothes, for example, or crafting rare items). Yet this is only user content on the micro level. In role-playing games, we have seen the first moves toward allowing users to change content on a macro scale. This is primarily done through large-scale warfare, an approach to high-end game design initiated in Mythic Entertainment's *Dark Age of Camelot (DAOC)*. In *DAOC*, there are three realms who fight for control of the frontier dividing them. If a realm is successful, certain benefits go to all members of that realm. This incites hundreds if not thousands of players to head out to the frontier to keep their own realm safe and powerful. By tracing the ebb and flow of these wars, a player can observe a political history of his world, and history that changes according to what the players do. This kind of faction warfare has been deployed with success in other games and is an important aspect of user-created content.

It is worth noting that such player versus player (PvP) systems are not critically dependent for their success on the skills of individual users, as micro content-creation is. Rather, all that's needed is a core game design within which it is entertaining for users to entertain other users. Tournament handicap golf is an example of good PvP design: The handicaps allow all of the players a chance to be in the running. Collectively, the players are going to write a history in the course of the tournament, with ups and downs all the way to the end. Virtual-world design is moving in that direction as well, with PvP content becoming the norm rather than the exception. Increasingly, the player base as a whole will be given more control over the relevant history of the world.

EASY INTERFACES

Finally, it should be noted that the game industry constantly works to make games easier to play. It is a strong norm in the industry to make the first 30 minutes of play an absolutely outstanding experience. Yet this is the time period when the player is first coming to grips with the interface. It follows that a great deal of attention has to be placed on interface design. Moreover, as games increasingly penetrate mainstream culture, the interface needs of a typical gamer are changing. If it is true that 25 percent of people over age 50 play video games, then it must also be true that at least some games should respect the needs of people who may wear bifocals or have arthritis. As games draw the attention of busy moms and dads, it becomes more and more risky to casually assume that every player has the time to poke around looking for the "Grenade" key.

We can expect that every aspect of game complexity will become easier over time, either because the interfaces become standardized and simplified, or because such complexity becomes a normal part of childhood, like riding a bike. The steepest learning curves in the industry are in virtual-world games, and that most certainly puts a limit on their use and penetration. Yet *World of Warcraft*'s interface represents a significant streamlining and simplification relative to the virtual worlds that preceded it, and it has enjoyed by far the greatest mainstream penetration of any. This predicts that the future belongs to games that are simple to use at first and grow in complexity with the user's interest.

THE FUTURE OF VIRTUAL WORLDS

From the beginning, people thinking and writing about cyberspace and virtual reality—William Gibson, Neal Stephenson, Ted Nelson, Vernor Vinge, Orson Scott Card, Howard Rheingold—have all explored concepts I have used here. Yet while these writers painted the picture, they generally did not put a time stamp on it. In the 1990s, there was much enthusiasm about virtual reality and a sense that it was just around the corner. Whether it is or not depends on your frame of reference. I believe we can expect to see all the advances mentioned here implemented within a generation.

CHAPTER FOUR

MIGRATION

My explorer mindset is well-suited to investigating virtual worlds, but such exploration also carries with it an assumption that there is a frontier, a line beyond which things are unknown. To be an explorer means there must be places out there that I have not yet seen. As a result, I will always have the option of leaving the places and people that I do know, and going off to explore these new regions that I don't know. I am not alone in this sense of frontier. Many of these regions are unknown to us all. In the old days, we might have said that they were "undiscovered territories"—hubris, the truth being that the territories were only undiscovered by us. Plenty of humans already lived in the allegedly New World happened upon by Christopher Columbus. Not so with new virtual worlds. On the day of launch, these are truly newly created terrains that no human has yet experienced.

We know from the past that the existence of frontiers makes a difference in how society operates. We know quite a bit about why people migrate, why human populations shift their location. The virtual-world migration will be different from ones that have come before, but no less significant.

IS CYBERSPACE A FRONTIER?

First things first: Why should we think of virtual worlds as frontiers? Michael J. Vlahos wrote of the Internet as a legitimate social and political territory as early as 1998.[1] Interestingly, Vlahos' area of expertise is not the Internet but international affairs; he is a scholar whose life work has been to understand tensions between states. A primary cause of international tensions today is the constant and fluid emergence of new power nodes as a result of uneven economic development. As such, we can expect an expert in international affairs to speak with some authority about the emergence of new social, political, and economic resources, and the stresses that may result. How interesting then to read his thoughts about the Net:

> Communication networks established by advances in informational technology create a "place," called the Infosphere, in which people form new social, political and employment arrangements. The creation of this place amounts to a major change in human history. The challenge for society and its leaders is to ensure the Infosphere is not a threat to standard of living but a place in which standards can improve.

The passage of time works to our advantage: We can now see the forms that the alleged Infosphere will take, and test them directly against our notions of what a frontier would be.

According to historian Frederick J. Turner, writing in 1893, the essential qualities of the frontier as it relates to a country like America, and by extension Europe, were "the existence of an area of free land, its continuous recession, and the advance of American settlement westward."[2] The Internet provides all these things, a point made in 2000 by Internet theorist Jeffrey R. Cooper.[3] The "free land" on the Internet is not exactly free, as we all know, but the land in the American West was not free either. It had to be taken, developed, and settled, in conflict against indigenous peoples as well as the laws of nature. What made the land of the West "free" was not absence of development cost, but the right to develop. There was enough "unexplored" land that anyone who wanted to explore could do so. Similarly, in virtual worlds the user can explore at will, and as world-building middleware becomes more ubiquitous, every user can develop new synthetic worlds. This frontier is also continuously receding. When a game world's servers get too crowded, the game's owners simply put another server online. New worlds are being developed and deployed continuously. Moreover, as user creation becomes an important element of the market, the amount of unexplored territory will rise dramatically as millions and millions of amateurs begin to craft their own pet worlds. Finally, as we have seen, this frontier experiences advancing settlement. People are using the new territories, and their use involves some separation from the old world.

Cooper's argument fits well in the case of virtual worlds. If we wanted to identify a candidate location for Vlahos' Infosphere, this would be it.

ECONOMICS OF MIGRATION

John Hicks, an eminent economist of the early twentieth century, wrote in his *The Theory of Wages* that "differences in net economic advantages, chiefly differences in wages, are the main causes of migration."[4] His followers today rely on the basic notion of wage rate differentials as the driving force of human migration. According to economist George Borjas, "Workers calculate the value of the opportunities available in each of the alternative labor markets, net out the cost of making the move, and choose whichever option maximizes the net present value of lifetime income."[5]

These economists are focusing only on wage differences, but their point is more general than that. Hicks writes of "economic advantages" in general, and then refines the notion to differences in wages. Similarly, Borjas speaks first of "the value of opportunities" and then refines the argument down to a maximization of lifetime income. Both speak first about something very general in the way of human happiness, but then focus on wages and income as the main subject. It is a deft move, from happiness down to income; we are after all dealing with technologies that focus strongly on happiness independently of any income or wage effects.

Economists believe that human behavior can be best modeled by a very general notion called "utility." When we see people pursue things more or less reasonably, we can model their behavior by saying that they are pursuing a thing called "utility" in general, to which the specific actions contribute. Thus if a woman gets up and goes to work, earning $100 for a day's labor, we say that the $100 must have increased her utility— otherwise she would not have done it. By observing all of the things people choose to do or not do, we can derive a general mapping of the value of choices, a "utility function."

Economists take the "utility function" as a kind of general behavioral score. Anything that a person might desire and pursue is a thing that counts as an aspect of the economic notion of utility. This is the level of generality at which Hicks and Borjas are operating when they refer to economic advantages and opportunities: They are referring to anything that would raise utility. That would include anything that would make a person better off according to her utility function, which is to say, anything that she might pursue or want, for whatever reason.

Thus the term "economic advantage" used by these economists is more general than it seems; it does not refer exclusively to money. In fact, economists have used utility theory to study all kinds of things that have nothing to do with money: safety, education, green space, time, anything we can imagine as contributing to a better life. The economic theory of migration applies to much more than wage differences.

Nonetheless, it helps if we focus on one source of differences, and wages are a decent stand-in for quality of living in general. If wages are higher in one country than another, all else equal, workers in the low-wage country will want to move to the high-wage country so long as the extra wages they can expect to earn there are greater than the cost of the move. This kind of model is very helpful in predicting behavior between two roughly comparable countries, because in comparable countries, the "all else equal" assumption is roughly true. It is still helpful, though less so, when we are talking about two countries at very different levels of development. In such cases, other differences in the quality of life have to be taken into account. So perhaps Blookistan has a slightly higher wage than Ferdonia, but a much better, and free, public education system. Perhaps the education system differences and not wages are the main driver of migration patterns; in any case, education system differences would have to be taken into account in order to isolate the effect of wage differences, and vice versa. Meanwhile, the analysis would also have to take into account every other significant quality of life difference in the two countries. Maybe Ferdonia has a better climate, while Blookistan has a more welcoming and open culture. All of these things enter into the utility functions of potential migrants; they all matter to them and might affect behavior.

What does this boil down to? Simple: People will move if it is better for them to do so. If you want to understand why people move from Ferdonia to Blookistan, analyze the overall quality of life in the two locations. Applied to synthetic worlds, that would imply that we need to compare the quality of life here in the real world to that available in the synthetic world. In the economic theory of migration, it would be "irrational"—*dumb*—for someone to spend time in the real world when the synthetic world offered a better quality of life. Furthermore, since we assume that people are not generally dumb, we must assume that those who choose to move to cyberspace are choosing the better option *for them*. We may disagree with their choice, but economists generally argue that it is a waste of time to dispute why people make the choices they do. Rather, our analysis should begin by assuming that people are just not stupid, that they generally know what they are doing, and that if they buy more potatoes than kidney beans, potatoes must just be the right choice for them, all things considered. Let the philosophers debate whether spuds are "better" than beans; economists don't care what people "ought" to do, they only care what they *do* do. People spend time in synthetic worlds. For those people, that's the right choice. The synthetic world offers them something good that the real world does not. Or, the real world is putting them through bad experiences that the synthetic world doesn't. For whatever reason, fantasyland is better. That's why people move there.

In what ways might the virtual world be better for someone? First, there's wages. Generally, the wages available in virtual worlds are pretty low, $1 to $4 hourly. On the other hand, talk about great working conditions! You get paid while playing a video game. That's already an attractive wage and amenities package for many people. And the cost of living is low—getting a new car or a horse or a faster means of travel in most virtual worlds is a matter of about $5 to $10 in real money.

Things might be better socially and culturally as well. In the real world, not everyone lives in a nice neighborhood with a loving family. In the virtual world, every neighborhood is pleasant, interesting, or fun. And while not everyone is loving, the dynamics of getting along with people certainly are different. No one can see your real skin color or body shape, so they can't be mean to you along those lines, as they often are in the real world. Activities in the virtual world are often designed to force people to make teams, too. Someone who is lonely in the real world, mostly because they have trouble making that first contact, doesn't have to worry in virtual worlds, because people are often thrown together by various missions and quests. Culturally, the real world can be a terribly empty place. Not everyone lives in a community with rich traditions, faiths, and stories that put meaning into everyone's life, whereas in synthetic worlds, everyone is asked to complete quests, fight enemies, and become a hero. On top of all this, synthetic worlds are designed to be fun all the time. The real world isn't. If you just like fun, the synthetic world is an attractive place. There are lots of reasons why certain people might find the synthetic world simply better than the real world.

When you think of the exodus to the virtual as the result of sane people choosing the world that's better for them, another aspect of this entire situation starts to stand out: This is a competition. People compare the real and the virtual, and then they decide. Usually, analysts writing about these choices tend to focus on the virtual side: how strange it is, how illusionary, fantastic, odd, challenging, escapist. What they don't focus on is the real side and its features. But this is wrong. If someone chooses potatoes over kidney beans, it's not right to put all the blame or praise on the features of the potato. The features of the kidney bean matter, too. The state of the real world is a critical element in the choices people are making. If the real world is not a very good place to live, then people will leave it. This, then, creates pressure on the people who run the real world to make it better. When two worlds are in competition, migration from one to the other will force the country that's losing people to change, adapt, improve.

When people are voting with their feet, their decisions affect both the target country and the source country. Migration tends to equalize living conditions across the places the migrants are leaving and the places they are entering. In the case of real and synthetic worlds, reality will be a constant invading pressure in virtual worlds, something we have seen already in the blurring of boundaries—people using real money to buy coins in a fantasy game, for example. But this also means that fun will be a constant invading pressure in the real world. The real world will be forced to become more like a fantasy game? Unbelievable. Yet that is precisely what any rational model of migration would predict. As the virtual exodus proceeds, the real world cannot remain the same.

ATTENTION

Some critics might reject the possibility of an exodus into the virtual simply because the body can't actually leave the real world at all. Every study of human migration so far has dealt exclusively with people moving their bodies from one place to another, permanently. With virtual worlds, however, we have people moving their attention, not their bodies, and they are moving back and forth all the time. Some people are present in multiple worlds at the same time; they just log in to several different worlds using different accounts on different computers. Or, all those computers can be used to log in to several accounts in the same world, in which case the player is present in one world as multiple characters. Sometimes, people will play as a team, other times, they play alone. Their bodies are never in the worlds at all, however, so the whole idea of *presence* is strange.

How does this fracturing of presence alter the notion of migration? We probably just need a new term. We should call the old-style migration, which was one-way, "discrete migration." The new-style migration, which is back and forth, fluid, should be called "continuous migration." With these terms, all we need is a slight modification or two, and all of the things we've learned about migration will still make sense in the real/virtual case.

One very simple modification that makes the migration approach applicable to the virtual exodus is to reduce moving costs to zero. Discrete migration has so far been the dominant kind studied because the costs of moving are so high in the real world. It tends to be a one-way affair. But with virtual worlds, we observe that the cost of sending a presence into an online game is pretty low, almost zero once you get things set up. Sure, with high moving costs, a migration approach deals mainly with discrete moves. With low moving costs, a migration approach deals with continuous moves but operates in precisely the same way. People move when the quality of life where they are is not as nice as in the other place. When the cost of moving is low, they move back and forth constantly as the comparisons change. Since the grass is always greener on the other side of the fence, we might expect that when moving is cheap, people do lots of moving. The dynamic is always the same: the individual considers where things are better, and goes there.

If people tend to prefer Blookistan's cuisine to Ferdonia's, the total amount of time people spend in Blookistan will exceed the total amount of time spent in Ferdonia. People still switch when they get bored with what they are eating, but they take a little longer to switch away from Blookistan—it is yummier. Then, because they are losing dining patrons to Blookistan, the Ferdonians have an incentive to improve their cooking. The migration of taste buds, though continuous, still puts pressure on Ferdonia to adapt. The migration of attention to virtual worlds, though continuous rather than discrete, will put pressure on the real world to adapt as well.

What about the lack of physicality? The body does not migrate at all in virtual worlds. But that is not all that important, given the receding impact of the body in the economy. Management experts Thomas Davenport and John Beck make the case that the truly scarce resource in the Information Age is not ideas or talent or physical presence but attention.[6] Our ability to produce things for others to read, listen to, or watch has skyrocketed, but our ability to do the reading, listening, and watching is fixed. The critical task for people today is to decide where their attention should be spent. Paying attention to task A over task B is just like "moving" to realm A and doing the job that is available there. If the chooser prefers to work on task B, she can go live in realm B for awhile. Right now I have several tasks that I could do: write this book, answer e-mails, make phone calls, or assist a colleague in learning how to sell things in Norrath, the fantasy world of *EverQuest*. The first job lives in Microsoft Word, the second in Mozilla Thunderbird, the third in my phone, and the fourth in *EverQuest*. Where will I go for the next half hour? Obviously, I stayed here. I didn't vote with my feet, I voted with my eyes. The eyes, say the prophets, are the windows to the soul; they reveal where attention is being paid. "The eyes don't lie," say Davenport and Beck. In the Information Age, where you are is where you are looking. Gaze is location. *Gaze migration* is attention migration, and it will be the source of many adaptation pressures for the real world.

THE THEORY OF TIME ALLOCATION

Gary Becker's theory of time allocation, which I mentioned briefly in the introduction, dates from 1965.[7] Addressing the then-recent declines in work weeks, he wrote: "The allocation and efficiency of non-working time may now be more important than that of working time; yet the attention paid by economists to the latter dwarfs any paid to the former."[8]

He went on to deliver a theory of how people allocate time to things other than work. It was important to do this, he argued, because work had come to occupy much less of our attention, relative to a past in which people who were not sleeping were usually working to obtain the bare minimum needs for survival. What we do with our nonwork time contributes just as much or more to our material well-being as working. This has implications for economists' basic model of choice. Previously, the focus had been almost entirely on money: An individual was said to earn a certain income from work, and that income had to be allocated among various money expenditures: new shoes for the kids, a car payment, broccoli. The choice model expanded to include what had become some very relevant considerations involving the time necessary to conduct any of these activities. Anyone who has tried to buy shoes for children knows that it takes up much more time than car payments or broccoli. That time cost, Becker argued, should be considered part of the price. By extension, the time spent at work is also something that has to be chosen, although here the "price" is negative: Work is the one commodity whose purchase brings money into the household. The point was that buying shoes and working were comparable activities, economically speaking. They changed utility, they changed money resources, and they changed time resources.

In the conclusion to his paper, Becker noted: "For example, a rise in earnings . . . would induce a decline in the amount of time used at consumption activities, because time would become more expensive."[9] This is a perfect description of the dynamics behind migration in an attention economy. It says that an increase in the amount of money a person can earn at work ("earnings") makes time "more expensive" (it makes it more costly in terms of income for a person to do something other than working). If my hourly pay is $10, it can be said that it "costs" me $10 to clock out early and spend the hour at the golf range. If my hourly pay rises to $20, that time at the range costs me twice as much in terms of earnings. When wages rise, the cost of doing anything other than work goes up. In response, Becker surmises, a rational person would reduce the amount of time spent in things other than work, the "consumption activities." This means, at a wage of $20 per hour, you might cut out of work to go to the range maybe only two days a week instead of five. If we remove the physicality inherent in the example I just gave, we get very close to a migration model for virtual worlds. Suppose, that is, that this person works in a call center but he enjoys a golf game on his work computer. Any time he is not taking calls, he is losing income, and the system doesn't let him do calls and play computer golf at the same time. At any one time, his eyeballs are going to look at incoming calls or the virtual greens, and he can switch costlessly between them. Becker's theory predicts that his decisions will depend on what he gets from working (the wages) and what he gets from the game (the fun). The dynamic mix of fun and money will send him back and forth over time, just as if he were "moving" between the realms of work and game.

The upshot: Almost no matter how you think about it, no matter what kind of logic you apply, you get the conclusion that people will move their attention in response to the things they experience in the separate realms of the real and the virtual. Not a radical idea by itself; it just has the radical implication that the real world and the virtual world will face pressures to converge.

WHICH CAME FIRST, THE SOCIETY OR THE GAME IT PLAYS?

Just because the virtual exodus creates these pressures doesn't necessarily mean that the real and the virtual will become more similar. A country without mountains cannot become a country with them. Can the virtual world become more like the real world? Can the real world become more like the virtual?

To reflect on these questions, consider the following:

> Like all the men of Babylon, I have been proconsul; like all, I have been a slave. I have known omnipotence, ignominy, imprisonment . . . I owe that almost monstrous variety to an institution—the Lottery—which is unknown in other nations, or at work in them imperfectly or secretly. I have not delved into this institution's history. I know that sages cannot agree. About its mighty purposes I know as much as a man untutored in astrology might know about the moon. Mine is a dizzying country in which the Lottery is a major element of reality . . . My father would tell how once, long ago—centuries? years?—the lottery in Babylon was a game played by commoners.
> —Jorge Luis Borges, *The Lottery in Babylon* (1962)

Borges' story goes on to relate how the Lottery changed from being a simple game among the poor to an infinite game of chance that regulated everything that happened in Babylon. Moreover, because of the need for control that a lottery demands, the construction and execution of the Lottery and its effects became secret. In the end, it became impossible to discern whether any given event or happenstance in Babylonian society was the result of chance, or of the Lottery. The social world and the game merged seamlessly.

Borges' Lottery echoes an earlier writer:

All the world's a stage, and all the men and women merely players.
—Shakespeare, *As You Like It,* Act II, Scene 7

These ideas challenge us to reflect on the extent to which the "real" world, this thing I have been distinguishing from the "virtual" world of the video game, in fact plays out like a big game itself. For example: Two students work for a landscaping company; they are assigned to work on different houses. One is hired by his homeowner to build some shelves, and there receives advice about careers that leads to an MBA and vast sums of wealth. The other student weeds the garden and goes home. If the allocation of the students to the houses were the result not of chance but of a secret game, how would the students know?

Indeed, they could not, because the outcome of a society looks exactly like the outcome of an open-ended multiplayer game. The people/players had various allocations of things at the beginning and other allocations at the end; they had paths through the experience that sometimes ran together and sometimes ran apart; they allied with one another and fought with one another; they thought quite a bit about what to do; they strategized and chose; fortune/the Lottery played with their choices and gave them outcomes and new situations/puzzles to consider. Society's basic structure is so very much like an open-ended multiplayer game that an entire branch of social science, game theory, is devoted to analyzing many social interactions as if they were actually very abstract strategic games. In game theory, we approach a national election not as a great moment of politics, but as a game in which the candidate with the most votes "wins." Game theorists do this because it makes it easier to understand incentives and outcomes in real elections. But perhaps this approach works as well as it does primarily because the election really is a game. The same could be said for many other social institutions. It is hard to look at society and determine which things are games and which things are not.

In the end, the question of whether virtual worlds and the real world are tailored from a similar pattern boils down to the question of whether virtual worlds are "real" or "genuine" in some sense. We do not have dragons in the real world, but the dragons are not what matters. What matters is which realm, real or virtual, is receiving more of our time and attention. This is determined by the amenities and wage structures in the two realms. Dragons are an amenity the real world cannot offer, but the absence of dragons does not negate the plausibility that people judge the amenities and incomes of the two realms to decide how to spend their time. So long as both realms offer something positive, and so long as those offerings can change, we will move back and forth between them.

As attention moves back and forth between game worlds and the real world, the migrating individual is constantly reminded of how the two worlds differ. In this, a situation of continuous migration carries more energy for change than a discrete migration. The migrant is not trapped forever in the destination realm, reporting back only in letters and phone calls. Rather, he can instantly recognize, judge, and express opinions about how one of the worlds should improve. If those opinions are ignored, he moves away. Instantly.

PART TWO

A POLICY ANALYSIS OF GAME DESIGN

CHAPTER FIVE

IN SEARCH OF AN UNDERSTANDING OF FUN AND GAMES

I f we were to survey the entire literature on fun and games, we would find that most of it is conceptual: broad, philosophical, cultural, aesthetic.[1] If we're trying to predict how the virtual world is going to change the real world, however, we need to be more concrete than this. It is really fascinating to read that virtual worlds are fun, and that Socrates thinks fun is important (which he does, by the way). But this doesn't answer the questions we need answered right now. What exactly are virtual worlds doing with, or to, the people who use them? How much of that action can we expect to see in the real world? For a policy analysis of fun we need to move from cultural studies to behavioral science; from aesthetics and philosophy into economics and psychology.

Economics has some very basic problems handling a concept like fun. First, economics is often called the queen of the social sciences, and in matters of policy analysis we generally turn to economics first for answers. But if we turned to economics right now with our policy questions about virtual worlds, we'd risk getting some very wrong answers. So we need to spill ink over the (missing) economics of fun and games, so as to warn people away from relying on economics until it gets a better handle on the issues. The second reason for sketching out the problems is to provide a roadmap for figuring things out. Economics is weak on fun today, but it doesn't have to stay that way. While most readers of this book are not economists (lucky you!), all of them will eventually be caught up in a general conversation about what to do when virtual worlds start affecting homes and workplaces and governmental affairs. Economists will be called on as experts. It would help the experts if the other people in the conversation have a sense of the analytical problems that fun provokes.

To see how the analysis of fun can go from being a matter for philosophers only, to being something we all have to care about, consider the example of reading. When reading was confined to a thin slice of people at the top of society, it was important in some sense, but had a fairly stable and minimal effect on how society operated. After the invention of the printing press, reading gradually became something that everyone could do. After books came journals and pamphlets and newspapers. Soon, everyone was reading all the time. If you couldn't read, you couldn't participate in society very well. If you didn't understand reading and its effects on the way people think and act, you couldn't understand why certain articles in the media or certain books had the effects that they did. Reading went from something nobody needed to worry about, to something everybody needed to worry about. I predict that the practice of spending time in virtual worlds will follow the same path from irrelevance to relevance.

To understand that path we have to try to understand fun, and the first thing we need to realize is that fun is hard to understand. Let's make the move that would seem the logical next step: let's look to the queen of the behavioral sciences, economics, and see what it has to say.

ECONOMICS AND FUN

There's something strange about economics as a field. It's been called "the dismal science" for eons, and most people I talk to recall economics as one of their most hated courses in school. That's odd, because economics has actually devoted many pages to the subject of human happiness. Economics respects the agency of single individuals who, we presume, doggedly pursue their own well-being. There is a whole subfield called "welfare economics" that does nothing but study the nature of individual and social well-being, through "objective functions." These "objective functions" are neutral, mathematical expressions of the desires of people, and what economists study with them is the extent to which people achieve what they want in life. Measurements are made at the individual level, determining whether a given policy will lower a particular type of person's "utility" (the numerical score given by the objective function). Measurements are also made at the social level, determining what fraction of a population loses utility when a policy goes into effect. Economists quantify these effects and monetize them, finding that, say, construction of a new highway will save drivers an amount of time worth $100 million. In the course of a career, an economist grapples with the notion of human well-being thousands of times. Because of economists' vast experience with happiness, their books ought to be hilarious, or exciting, or sexy—anything that raises the reader's utility. You would think, with all that wisdom about human happiness, economists would have long since figured out how to make their field the funnest thing going. But we know the truth.[2] Apparently when we economists come to our word processors for the first time, all respect for the reader's well-being apparently flies out of mind, never to return. Writing proceeds with all the elegance of shards of broken glass being raked across cobblestone.

The explanation lies in the economist's notion of well-being. When economists say someone is "better off," they do not necessarily mean that the person is happier. Well-being is not the same thing as a notion of happiness, or joy, or fun. Well-being, according to economics, is achieved when an individual attains her goals, whatever they may be. A suicidal person may have the goal of killing herself, which she can achieve several different ways. The economist would take her goal as given—inducing her own death quickly and painlessly—and then determine which of the methods—for example, slicing wrists or hanging—was least costly in terms of expected suffering. If the suicidal person felt that hanging was better, and if she then hung herself, the economist would proclaim that she had maximized her well-being. If before committing the deed she obtained something that would make her death even quicker and less painful—a gun—the economist would assert that she had become better off. Her goal of a quick, painless suicide had become easier to attain; she had moved closer to the goals she set out for herself; the utility score produced by her objective function would become a higher number. In this scenario, we can see that her well-being as measured by economists has little to do with her emotional state. She is very sad the whole time, and no less sad when she gets the gun. Perhaps she is more sad. Her "well-being" goes up when she finds the gun, but she is no closer to joy.

Economists don't know much about happiness because they focus on choices and rationality, not emotional states. Most times, a person's rational choices will indeed lead them to happiness. On the other hand, sometimes we have objectives that we know will lead us to misery.[3] The language of "better off" and worse off" that economists use certainly sounds like it is pointing to emotional states. But it just isn't.

THE POLICY INADEQUACY OF
ECONOMIC WELL-BEING

This has implications for the way we discuss policies. We are entering an era in which public policy will be asked to make people happy, often by making society more fun. We will turn to economics, the paradigm we usually use to analyze public policy, and it will have little or nothing to say. The absence of relevant information, however, will be very hard for most people to see, including most economists. Economists will speak, and people will listen. But I predict that the policies chosen will doggedly make people "better off," not *happier.* In fact, many policies that make people "better off" will make them *unhappy.* In those cases, if we were to then turn to economists and say, "Modify your policies to correct this situation," they would not be able to come up with a solution. Not because they don't want to, but because they can't. Economics has not just overlooked happiness; it has built an entire intellectual structure within which it is impossible to see the joy of choosing, a particular aspect of happiness that comes up every time someone is having fun.

Let's consider a specific situation. Fred works for an insurance company. At night, he plays the stock market through a discount brokerage firm. His goal is to buy a red Corvette convertible and put a bumper sticker on it that reads COURTESY OF DOW JONES. To meet that goal, he is saving money from his stock market activities. The car costs $25,000. In his mind, Fred thinks of each dollar he makes trading stocks as being worth 1/25,000 of a car, so that if he wins $5,000 on a given night, he exults "I just made one-fifth of my red hot car." An economist would agree that each such dollar earned increases his well-being, getting him closer and closer to that car.

Now if the government turned a charitable eye toward Fred, it might ask the economist for advice on how to help him. After all, here he is, struggling to get this car, but still thousands and thousands of dollars away from it. The economist, focused on the economic notion of well-being, might say "Give Fred a $10 tax break to help him buy the car." Such a gift would unquestionably raise Fred's well-being: It would get him $10 closer to the car. Or, you might say that Fred would perceive the tax break as a gift of 10/25,000 of a car, courtesy of Uncle Sam. Either way, this would be the standard policy approach to this problem: Fred has a goal that he hasn't reached, so give him help toward that goal, and his well-being will go up—a good thing.

Suppose, however, that the government became zealous in its drive to help Fred, giving him a tax break not of $10 but of $25,000, and then requiring that he use it to buy the car. If $10 was good, must not $25,000 be better? And he wants the car, so let's give him the car. The economist would have to say that this would raise Fred's well-being, because the $25,000 would certainly get Fred to his goal. But would this gift make Fred happy? On the one hand, he would get the car. That's very good. But what about the bumper sticker? He can't really have one that says COURTESY OF DOW JONES now; he can't brag about the car as his achievement from being a great trader. The correct bumper sticker would read GOVERNMENT HANDOUT. The loss of the Dow Jones label takes away considerably from Fred's happiness at getting the car. He is happier, sure, but not as happy as if he had earned the car on the stock market. Indeed, for the sake of concreteness, let's say he feels only $20,000 happier.

In terms of welfare economics, we would say that Fred *discounts* the government payment: The payment is $25,000 but produces only $20,000 worth of happiness. One study, by economist Robert Moffitt, found this discounting effect for cash aid payments to needy mothers.[4] The aid recipients treated a dollar of aid income as being worth less than a dollar. To put it another way, if dollars could come from two sources, one of them earnings and the other aid, they would prefer to have 90 cents of the earnings dollar over the entire aid dollar.

These examples show that responding to someone's problem by solving it for them can discount the positive effect the action is supposed to have. Moffitt associated this discounting with stigma—the recipients, he argued, were probably ashamed to get aid. Fred's discounting, conversely, relates to the way he wants to reach his goals. He was playing a little game with himself and the world, challenging himself to be a good trader and make a lot of money, promising to reward himself for the effort with a big flashy car. This game was wrecked when the government gave Fred the prize for doing nothing. In cost-benefit terms, this policy was a $5,000 mistake: It cost the government $25,000 but only created $20,000 in happiness.

Despite being a mistake, this kind of policy is the one that a strict economic approach always recommends. If you see a problem, the prescription goes, help people solve it. This overlooks the very real possibility that the people view solving the problem as essential to their self-esteem. There's joy in overcoming challenge. There's a happiness in choice. If you solve people's problems for them, you might be making them miserable. True, in some cases, people would rather just get their problems taken care of. There's no fun in filling a pothole by yourself. Filling a pothole, however, is not a fun game.

It's when public policy starts to get involved with fun and games that this problem of economics really hits home. Imagine if a puzzle maker went to an economist and asked for advice:

> Puzzle maker: "People say my puzzle is no fun. How can I improve it?"
> Economist: "When people use your puzzle, what is their objective? What are their constraints?"
> Puzzle Maker: "Their objective is to solve the puzzle, to put the pieces together in the right way. The constraint is that the puzzle is cut up into 100 pieces."
> Economist: "Easy. Reduce the number of pieces to just two. That will allow everyone to achieve their objectives rapidly, which will maximize their well-being."

This is not very good advice.[5]

When happiness and well-being are in conflict like this, it becomes clear that the core objective of public policy should be to promote happiness, not well-being. This dovetails with arguments by some highly respected welfare economists. Amartya Sen has argued that we need to focus on the direct experiences of people, not merely the extent to which they achieve their own goals.[6] Sometimes, helping people find happiness may involve something other than giving them the things they currently seek. What we have discovered here is a new strategy for welfare economics, one founded on the joy of choosing. What if policy focused on redesigning the problem environment so that it better induces happiness? It would mean trying to change the problem so that when people work their way through the challenge themselves, they feel happier. Under this approach, the essence of public policy is not really problem solving, it is game design. The best policy is not always to take people out of their problems. The best policy is to make problems more rewarding to solve.

In the case of Fred the stock broker, a game design approach would suggest buying him better Internet connections and more computer screens so he can trade on even thinner margins. Fred would win his little game more quickly, but he would retain the satisfaction of getting the car himself. Or, the government could add $10,000 worth of snazzy modifications to the car, making Fred's prize ride really special. That too would raise Fred's well-being while keeping him happy in his game.

A game design approach to public policy would be a radical departure from the status quo. But I predict we will not have a choice. The growing importance of fun will make it second nature for most people to see the answers to social problems as a simple matter of redesigning the rules of the game.

CHAPTER SIX

A THEORY OF FUN

Fun is a sensation, a feeling, an element of happiness. It includes the satisfaction of reaching goals, but also of having goals to reach and choices about how to reach them. Fun is also associated with games, especially digital games. Ask any kid why he spends so much time with video games, and he will answer "It's fun!" That's a vague reason, but we now have some tools, from game design and psychology, that will allow us to have a more concrete understanding of what is going on in someone's head when they say "That game was fun."

Let's begin with game designers. Raph Koster has written specifically on his theory of fun, and identifies it with the release of chemicals in the brain.[1] When you do something fun, you wash your brain with endorphins, which humans perceive as a positive thing. Since other sensations like pleasure and contentment also make us feel good by releasing endorphins, Koster equates all such things with fun; they are all different words for a single chemical event. Koster then argues that games trigger this chemical event through a specific kind of experience: mastery. When we are playing a game, he argues, we are unconsciously engaging an ages-old system of learning. We are trying to figure out a complex system. When we do, a mastery-moment happens, and the endorphins rush out. That is where the fun of games comes from.

Koster is right, but we can make his neurochemical approach even more specific. We can ground it in media psychology and thereby distinguish fun from happiness in general. Our version of fun will be a specific kind of happiness, associated with mental processes that involve both playing and survival. Because it is distinct from other forms of happiness, it can also get in the way of those other forms. People pursuing fun can put themselves at risk—as when a skier breaks his leg. The fun we will define happens all over the place, and we can use it to design not only games but also real-world policies.

VIDEO GAMES AND THE OLD BRAIN

The story of fun I am trying to tell begins in the brain, not with pleasure, but rather cognition. Over the past 15 years, media psychologists have developed a powerful core theory of how the brain responds cognitively to media. As already described in Chapter Two, in the mid-1990s, Byron Reeves and Clifford Nass conducted a series of experiments establishing that the core structures of the brain interpret media and reality in the same way.[2] The brain's basic structures evolved when there were no media. The earliest part of the brain, the "old brain," regulates basic processing and drives, including split-second decisions about what information is relevant and what can be ignored. Your higher thinking, your consciousness, is handled by later structures, the "new brain," the frontal lobes. The new brain understands the difference between a symbol and the thing it represents; the old brain does not. Because of this old brain/new brain structure, media processing follows a specific path. The old brain treats what it sees as absolutely real, unless and until the new brain steps in and says "No, that's just a picture on TV." The acknowledgement of difference between media and reality does not come from instinct. It rather is something we see, recognize, take note of, and process.

Distinguishing reality from symbol is not free. In fact, no act of cognitive processing is free. Processing is thinking, thinking requires mental resources, and therefore our processing of media is selective and incomplete.[3] We cannot notice every detail in our environment. Moreover, we will notice, understand, and retain media information according to how important it is judged to be by deeper motivational systems. Our response to media is motivated. A media image of a roaring dinosaur will be noticed because it represents a threat. The old brain does not yet realize, in the microseconds within which such decisions are made, that the dinosaur is not real. Receiving the first tidbits of the image from the corner of the eye, the old brain shouts "Look at that!" and the sensory system responds accordingly; eye and neck muscles move involuntarily. Receiving more of the image, the old brain shouts "That looks like something that could eat us! We'd better understand what it is and keep a copy in memory!" The processing and memory structures then get to work. Sometime after this, the frontal lobes check in with a reminder that the dinosaur was on TV and therefore not real. Nonetheless, it was observed, processed, and filed before the mind could judge its reality.

Annie Lang has extended this model to the specific subject of video games.[4] Lang's work focuses on the media functions of the old brain— the brain that does not know media are not real—and this enables her to invoke evolutionary and adaptive reasoning to explain how the brain operates. Motivation is the core concept: Why does the brain seek out stimuli? From an evolutionary perspective, there are two basic motivational systems, the appetitive and the aversive, both related to survival. Appetitive motivation makes us pursue things like food and sex—things in the environment that will help us and our genes survive. Aversive motivation makes us fight or run away from things that seem dangerous. In support of these ideas, Lang cites work by psychologist John T. Cacioppo, who has found that these two motivational dimensions represent completely independent systems.[5] The appetitive system activates when survival-related resources appear, whether there is a threat present or not. Similarly, when a threat appears, the aversive system kicks in, whether there are resources in play or not. *Coactivation* occurs when a resource is paired with a threat, such as when a tiger stands over a fresh kill.

Cacioppo and Lang believe that these motivational systems are more or less permanent in people, and therefore we can identify someone's basic mental make-up by examining what they do when no resources or threats are present. From an evolutionary perspective, one would want a person to have a slight positive bias in the appetitive system: If there is no current stimulus, go seek one. And there is evidence that human beings do have a slight *positivity offset* that is higher for some people than for others. Some people cannot sit still for a moment but must rush out and find a new stimulus, while others are far less interested in the new. Along the aversive dimension, there does not appear to be a significant offset, but there is some variation in how rapidly the aversive system responds to new stimuli. This is called *negativity bias,* and also is higher for some than for others. Some people get worked up immediately when they see danger, while others remain calm and collected. Lang and her colleagues have done empirical studies of the distribution of positivity offset and negativity bias in human populations and found that there are several classes of people:

- Risk takers: high positivity offset (PO) and low negativity bias (NB)
- Risk avoiders: Low PO and high NB
- Inactives: Low PO and Low NB
- Coactives: High PO and High NB

There is also a distinct relationship between these motivational systems and human emotions. For one thing, emotions come later: first, the brain processes a stimulus according to this motivational scheme, and only then do the emotion-generating structures get activated. Moreover, stimuli that engage the motivational system more powerfully will have a greater effect on the emotional system. When something good appears on the screen, the appetitive system kicks in and positive emotions are felt; if it is really, really good, the appetitive systems works harder and the emotions are more intense.

So how does this apply to video game play? Video games are media messages, and they are designed to frustrate any attempt by the new brain to contradict the old brain's presumption that this media environment is real. In other words, the game is designed to be so enjoyable and fun that you lose yourself in it. At those moments when the new brain might step in and say "Hey, this is not real" it instead holds its tongue, preferring not to burst your bubble. Because the fantasy just plain feels good, the new brain lets the old brain treat it all as real. Thus the other parts of the brain's work are largely premised on the reality of the game. Within that reality, the brain responds to resources and threats as it would here on Earth: Treasure chests activate the appetitive system, while large, angry, fire-breathing, winged creatures activate the aversive system. Dragons guarding treasures cause coactivation: fear and desire. Great big dragons on huge mounds of treasure cause intense coactivation: terror and money lust. Sandbox games—games that initially have nothing in them, because the player is supposed to build—are not a good match to people with low positivity offset, since in the absence of stimuli those folks will do nothing. Thrill seekers need to be in games where something new is coming every second, otherwise they get bored. The theory connects at many points to the practice of game design and to what we know about the effects of games on players.

THE PSYCHOLOGY OF HAPPINESS

A motivated cognition theory suggests that media in general, and video games in particular, grab our attention by presenting objects that are relevant to the basic motivation of any organism, namely, to survive. Emotions follow: terror for objects that appear immediately threatening, anxiety for such threats that seem low-grade but ominous, joy for overcoming threats—moments of mastery—and for acquiring resources, such as treasure or friends. If policy is to get better at helping people be happy, it would have to become more sophisticated at manipulating such objects in the real world as well as in media.

Clearly, it is a challenge to try to make people happy through manipulation of the social order. Yet this is precisely the challenge that virtual-world designers have faced and mastered. They have created entire social orders in which each person experiences an endless stream of motivation to action, and actions that have substantial consequences for emotion. Moreover, most of the time, the reigning and final emotions are satisfaction, joy, pleasure: variations on happiness.

To understand what game designers seem to have accomplished, let's look more deeply into the psychology of pleasure. In an encyclopedic 1999 volume, psychologists Daniel Kahneman, Ed Diener, and Norbert Schwarz sought to summarize everything then known about the psychology of human well-being.[6] In 600 pages, they sought to found what they called a new field named *hedonic psychology:* the study of what makes experience and life pleasant or unpleasant. They wrote of their belief that such a field would one day have genuine relevance for the way we structure our world:

> Our hope is that hedonic psychology will be relevant to policy. We recognize, with a large degree of humility, that scientific understanding in this field is currently woefully inadequate to provide a strong underpinning for national policies. We believe, however, that in the decades to come there will be much greater success in understanding hedonics, and that principles will emerge that can be used by policymakers.[7]

It is strange but true that these wishes have been realized in the game industry more than anywhere else. The important thing to stress in this quotation is its admission of how new the psychological study of happiness is.

But recent advances in this area have been rapid. Affective neuroscience and more recent psychological studies have learned much about where emotions come from.[8] German psychologist Stefan Klein's research indicates that positive and negative emotions come from different parts of the brain, and that there are specific things we can do to increase the amount of positive emotion we feel.[9] Physical exercise is one. But of greatest relevance for us here is Klein's finding that we can

EXODUS TO THE VIRTUAL WORLD

induce positive emotions by engaging in simple tasks that easily offer a sense of success. In other words, you can beat depression by playing video games with the difficulty level set to "easy."

Moreover, contrary to some earlier findings, it does seem possible to make people happier in general. There was a time when it was feared that happiness was a treadmill: Every time a person did something that improved their happiness—got a new house, won the lottery, remarried—they would then become used to that new thing, and their aspirations would rise to some higher level, making them unhappy again. However, newer research in hedonic psychology suggests that aspirations do not necessarily move this way; we are not caught on a hedonic treadmill.[10] This is clearly a fast-moving field, but the point is, joys, and probably fun too, can be obtained and even increased when a person's environment is correctly designed.

As for where happiness specifically comes from, biopsychologist Kent Berridge finds that pleasure is a gloss that gets painted on top of underlying brain functions.[11] Engaging this gloss is more complex than we might realize. Certain system triggers, like dopamine, do not always yield pleasure. Sweet things are supposed to yield pleasure, but if you got very, very drunk for the first time off of peppermint schnapps, you may acquire a lifelong aversion to the sweetness of peppermint. Moreover, the pleasure system activates differently for wants as opposed to likes. A "want" is a craving, a feeling that, if only you could expose yourself to this particular sensation, you would feel pleasure. A "like" is just plain happiness, a feeling being experienced that has the pleasure gloss on it. Usually, the want sensation points accurately at sensations that, once experienced, do yield pleasure. But not always.

Sometimes, and maybe so often as to explain the frequently farcical nature of human life, wants point to sensations that do not yield likes.

The addict craves but does not enjoy. Psychologist Daniel Gilbert has written about many of the apparently contradictory and counterintuitive ways that happiness occurs.[12] For example, most parents say they love their children and are happy to have them. Yet the day to day experience of taking care of children does not make us very happy. Three reasons for the apparent discrepancy:[13]

- The brain is trained to connect happiness and cost. We are used to the idea that the best things cost lots of money, so used to it that when we spend a lot of money to get something, we force ourselves to believe it is a good thing. Children cost us a lot of time and money, so the brain judges them positively.
- One powerful positive emotional experience is remembered over one million negative ones. Children have this habit of winning over your heart with a single word.
- We tend to assess pleasure by referencing what else is available. Parents raising young children can't do much else; the kids become the primary source of happiness.

Happiness is a trickster.

While tricky in general, though, happiness has some elements that can be induced reliably and as a constant stream of sensation. One example is "flow," introduced by psychologist and management professor Mihaly Csikszentmihalyi in 1990.[14] People find flow to be a very pleasurable sensation. It is described as being "in the zone," a state in which all attention is directed to the task at hand. Self-consciousness disappears. The individual feels utterly immersed, and skills are deployed at the highest level of mastery. The interesting thing about flow is that it occurs under certain specific conditions. Some of the critical elements for inducing flow are immediate feedback, a clear sense of objectives and failure states, and a challenge level that is not too easy or too hard. Easy tasks lead to boredom, which leads to a return to the reflective state and self-consciousness. Hard tasks lead to frustration, which similarly leads to self-consciousness and a breaking of the spell. This is a fairly stringent series of requirements, but also a reliable recipe. Do these things, and flow will happen. Happiness follows.

Happiness is clearly a mental system with its own unique features. But where does fun fit in? It is an aspect of happiness, in that people having fun are happy. But how exactly do fun activities lead to happy feelings?

HAPPINESS, PLAY, AND GAMES

To refocus on fun, we need to be more specific about the games and play that are said to produce it. Let's begin with play. According to those who think most deeply about it, play is an activity that emulates real-world activity but is not taken seriously.[15] It is make-believe. Play also has a critical role in mammalian survival: You play to prepare for real-world situations where simple mistakes could kill you.[16] That is why so much play is violent: In situations of real violence, a simple mistake is extremely costly. Better to make that mistake when trying to nip your daddy's ear. It won't mean death then. But play is used to acquire skill in nonviolent activities as well. Communications scholar Francis Steen stresses that for play to assist survival, it must be intrinsically rewarding. If we connect here to the psychology of happiness, winning at play must be a sensation that acquires the pleasure gloss by itself. Suppose kids are playing a game in which the reward is a cookie. If they win, the cookie tastes good, but the feeling of winning at play feels good too, and is a completely separate source of pleasure. Even if there were no cookie, the kids still feel good about winning. The pleasure gloss comes merely from playing, and doing so successfully. It rewards the act of play itself. Escaping from a real tiger is satisfying, but escaping from Daddy won't be, unless play in and of itself gives pleasure.

There's more to this than Darwinism. Psychologist Susan Blackmore argues that behaviors like play will thrive among humans if the behaviors can survive the process of cultural selection and evolution.[17] Blackmore believes that behaviors are like genes. Behaviors that people learn about, then copy, spread widely in a population. Behaviors that people don't end up copying die out. Play is one such behavior. It thrives on the Internet, the most powerful communication tool ever invented. It is engaging to newcomers and old veterans alike. It broadcasts its existence powerfully. Virtually everyone who encounters play receives pleasure frequently. Play is an easy-to-copy behavior that brings joy. It is not only explained by our need for biological survival, but also by the survival of behaviors in culture.

What about games? Games are not the same thing as play. Games are designed goal environments with uncertain outcomes. They are social institutions. It so happens that games are a perfect environment for creating play, but they also appear under other circumstances. Elections are clearly games. So are stock markets. And wars. All serious things, but they are all designed goal environments with uncertain outcomes.

Thus: Play is intense, survival-relevant action that's not serious. Games are designed goal environments with uncertain outcomes. How do these relate to happiness?

Certainly, games clearly label winning and losing states, and such states match directly to our activation systems: Winning excites the appetitive system, and losing excites the aversive system. Games are hugely useful to humanity in that they quickly take care of the otherwise massive processing task of figuring out whether a stimulus in the environment is a resource or a threat. It was easy in the jungle: Fangs meant threat, water meant resource. At a very early point, though, the mammalian brain acquired systems for deciding what to do about more complex stimuli. Some juicy berries are poisonous. As the environment in which we operate has become more complex, the task of associating experiences with threats and opportunities becomes gargantuan. Games simplify the task by clearly labeling victory and loss conditions. Our brains need only assess whether these conditions are somewhat accurate, by testing our motivation. Would it feel like a resource acquisition, were I to win this contest? Would it feel like succumbing to a threat to lose? If so, game on. That is, by engaging fully in the game, we take its victory and loss conditions as accurate indicators of our primal needs to survive. Such labeling also immediately sets the table for flow states to be engaged. Indeed, linking together games would be one way to make flow happen more or less continually, and perhaps explains why people can play for very long periods of time. Games provide the clear labeling of success and failure, the constant and immediate feedback, and the dynamic challenge adjustment that would allow a flow state to persist indefinitely.

In addition, the labeling of win/loss in place of primal needs is what makes games so effective at instituting play. Play serves its functions best when we think it is relevant to survival. When we play within the context of a game, the game labels the survival conditions quite clearly. The prehistoric ur-games Escape from Daddy, Get the Ball, and Where Am I?, do a wonderful job of connecting the goal outcomes of the game to practical matters of survival. The play impulse works very well in these contexts. Other attempted ur-games, such as Get Over Here by the Time I Count Three, and Put That Precious Object Down Right Now, do not work so well in a play context and have remained in the realm of the serious.

Happiness in games and play do stem from things like mastery, as Koster argues. We would understand Koster's mastery pleasure as a gloss applied to the sensation of learning the lesson that play is attempting to teach. In the context of games specifically, it is the joy of getting to the winning condition, because at that moment the game confirms to the player that a survival-essential skill has been mastered. Thus, even though fighting a terrible dragon would ordinarily be terrifying, once placed in the context of play, success versus the dragon generates waves of relief (as it would in the real world) along with waves of pleasure from winning (which the real world may or may not provide).

FUN: A DEFINITION

Putting all of these strands together, here's what I think fun is:

Fun is a pleasurable sensation attributed to an activity when:

1. the activity causes the coactivation of motivational systems,
2. the activity is (possibly metaphorically) relevant to survival,
3. the individual's choices promote survival, and
4. the situation is known to be play.

Beginning at the end, the definition proposes that fun only happens during play. Think of the times when you've heard someone say "Well, that was fun" in an ironic sense—usually it was after something that involved both threats and opportunities and survival-like conditions, but was altogether serious. Outside play, things are not fun, they are scary.

Survival is also relevant to fun. The second and third part of the definition say that fun is a pleasure that comes from winning at the game of evolutionary adaptation. As for survival, we know that aiding survival is the deepest purpose of play. So we conclude that a player's fun is enhanced when the activities she's doing are sensed to be relevant to survival. This works even if the association is metaphorical. So long as the actions the player is asked to do involve resource acquisition or threat avoidance, fun happens. And of course you have to win; part three stresses that it is not fun to lose. The fun feeling happens only when the actions being undertaken appear to be succeeding, reducing threats or gaining resources.

Finally, in part one, the definition proposes that fun occurs specifically under conditions of coactivation, that is, when both opportunities and threats exist. It is pleasurable, but not fun, to receive affection from an attractive potential mate. It is a relief, but not fun, to escape from life-threatening danger. What is fun is to rescue an attractive potential mate from the demon who has imprisoned her (so long as it is all play). Both the appetitive and aversive systems must be engaged at a similar level. Otherwise the player feels bored (too much appetitive activation) or frustrated (too much aversive activation). And the more strongly the two systems are engaged, the more intense the feeling of fun.

Fun is a part of happiness, a subset of all positive emotional states. Many forms of happiness can be distinguished from fun, in that they do not in general involve the activation of the aversive system. Moreover, many forms of happiness do not require that you do anything, whereas fun is an attribute of activity. A person can feel *satisfied* or *content* without having fun. Indeed, a person in pursuit of fun can do things that prevent later contentment. Fun is a sufficient condition for happiness, but not a necessary condition. Fun makes people happy in the moment it occurs.

More than any other feeling, fun is the mental state that games produce. Games are environments that quickly translate survival criteria into easily observed win-loss states, enabling fun to happen much more quickly. Games cut down the complexity of survival, reducing the situation to bare bones: The orc is bad, the Silver Chalice of Freeport is good, the orc must be killed to get the chalice. Very few mental resources have to go into processing these symbols. Compare that to the processing your mind has to do in order to decide whether a question posed by the boss or a client is important or not. All that processing leaves fewer resources for figuring out what to say. In a game, your mind has comparatively more resources to devote to the task of winning, which is also central to feeling happy about it all.

Fun exists in a balance between the heightened intensity that comes with more strenuous, more activating situations, and the requirement that nothing is *really* serious. This makes the design of fun difficult: You have to keep the player entertained and engaged by making the event seem very, very relevant to survival. But if it is too relevant, it risks being too serious. As a serious matter, it may be fruitful in numerous ways, but it won't be fun. A mountain-climbing trip is fun until Johnson breaks his leg and we have to get him out of there. We may learn a lot of climbing skills, but the whole thing isn't fun anymore. The seriousness of the event—its balance between survival and play—is a primary lever by which the amount of fun is manipulated.

The role of winning in fun explains why fun is evolutionarily important. The pleasure that gets attached to winning at fun is the psychological reward for doing well at play. Play involves dealing with play-threats so as to obtain play resources. Win at that game, and you're likely to do well against real threats when real resources are at stake. To give you a reason to try hard at your play, the system gives you some joy when you win.

Fun is related to flow: A linked sequence of activities that generate fun will also be generating flow. But you can have fun without being in a state of flow. For example, a group of players who collectively take on a dragon will each have fun, being coactivated by a situation with clear survival relevance, but until they know each other very well, they will probably not be able to lose all self-consciousness and enter "the zone." You can also experience flow without having fun. A runner can face a series of challenges with immediate feedback but have no sense that any of it is survival related. Also, some flow experiences are not play: A firefighter may enter flow while dousing flames. Usually, however, the fun in games is very tightly connected to flow. Games allow the linking of activities so that fun can become continuous, and this is what puts the player in a state of flow.

There are of course conditions in which fun may appear in real-life games that are not play, but note that this occurs only when the individual adopts a playful attitude. It is an interesting performance strategy, in fact. The trader who takes the market less seriously may start to have fun with his job, entering more easily into a state of flow that enables him to deploy his skills to better effect. Those who treat real life as play seem to enjoy it more. Perhaps they focus their minds primarily on situations in which threats and opportunities seem bundled together, trying to beat the former and grab the latter.

In this definition, we make fun concrete as a unique psychological reward mechanism. Fun comes from playing at killing the dragon and grabbing the Gilded Vessel. Interestingly enough, this is exactly what the vast majority of experience within virtual worlds turns out to be: a never-ending sequence of quests of the form "A terrible X is threatening a precious Y! The X's strength stems from a powerful Z! Go kill the X, save the Y, and you may keep the Y and the Z for yourself!" Players of virtual worlds experience fun more or less constantly: Kill the monster, get the treasure, use the treasure to become more powerful, kill a more powerful monster, get more valuable treasure, make yourself still more powerful, and so on and so on. When people say that virtual worlds are fun, they are not kidding. Virtual worlds are nothing but fun, by design.

POLICY IMPLICATIONS OF GAME DESIGN

The happiness policy sought by hedonic psychologists is still far from being implemented by any real-world government. Given the trickiness of the happiness mechanism, any general attempt to make people happier has to be done carefully. It would be helpful if there were some systems, methods, and approaches that were guaranteed to make most people happy, most of the time they engage with them.

I think that fun allows this kind of "assured-happiness" approach. It is a positive emotion that activates reliably under known conditions. Therefore, policy can focus on creating those conditions, on the assumption that once those conditions are put in place, fun will almost certainly happen. Since fun is an aspect of happiness, we would know that we are making people happy. Indeed if such fun-inducing conditions can be created as a sequence that extends through time, they would allow people to experience a more or less unbroken stream of positive feelings. In short, a deeper understanding of fun allows us to imagine a public policy environment that is devoted to human happiness in a practical, reliable way.

Does this seem fantastic? It isn't. In fact we do not need to *imagine* such a public policy environment. It already exists. It is known as *game design.*

CHAPTER SEVEN

VIRTUAL-WORLD DESIGN AS PUBLIC POLICY

G ame design seeks to make people happy through institutions of fun. Virtual-world design takes everything that game design does and embeds it in a community of people. That makes virtual-world design a form of public policy; designers create social orders. They make the rules by which a society operates. For example, a world designer can decide that players who possess a certain kind of wand can summon invisible eagles, and that those eagles can carry those players around the world at ten times the usual running speed. The world designer can then make the wand really hard to find. The net result will be a huge inequality in power. Those few people who have the wand can fly around in the sky, while the masses of people on the ground have to foot it. The choices a virtual-world designer makes cause the emergence of certain kinds of social structures: inequality, political power, prestige, beauty, reputations. Everything that makes up the social order happens as the result of real people reacting to the environment the designer creates, the rules he lays down. In the context of virtual worlds, game design is *equivalent* to public policy design. Game designers make the rules by which people play, in the same way that governments make the rules by which we all live. The designers are the sovereign. Never since Louis XIV has the maxim *l'etat, c'est moi* better fit a class of people; it should be the very motto of the International Game Design Association. Truly, in the world he makes, the designer is the Sun King. He can do anything.

Up to this point in history, the objective of most virtual-world designs has been to create good commercial games. When games were primarily single-player systems, the environments that designers made were basically toys. But once single-player games became massive online worlds, these *environments* for fun became *societies* for fun. The design task changed from making fun experiences to making fun social orders. This is a very different objective than real-world governments have, of course; for most of human history, governments have not had to think of entertaining the citizenry. But the goals of both are the same: Design a social order to some specifications. The social orders that have been designed by virtual-world creators have the flavor of real-world government, but since they are written to a different objective, they are different in structure. The emergence of virtual worlds in the commercial entertainment sector represents a fascinating experiment in social policy: a test of whether it is possible to create an entire society in which the primary goal of government is to help people have fun.

Game designers have learned much from their failures and even more from their successes. They have indeed been successful in designing societies where everyone has fun all the time, so much so that virtual worlds are now grabbing millions and millions of hours of attention. A veritable school of design practice has emerged and solidified. Certain design features have become common among all synthetic worlds. A blueprint for the generic fun society exists, not in the hallowed halls of Congress or Ivy League government departments, but in the cubicle warrens of game design companies.

We are witnessing the birth of a new science, the practical science of giving people the sensation of fun through the design of social institutions. This new science will play an ever more significant role in public affairs during the course of the twenty-first century. As the exodus to the virtual world proceeds, more and more people will come to view the tenets of this new science as practical rules for running the real world. Those tenets have already been developed, and at the moment, they are all rules of some game.

Let's call the new science fungineering. The term "fungineer" has been applied as a buzzword to a certain class of cultural creators in the realms of new media and entertainment. Here, though, the meaning intended is technical, applied, and specific:

> A *fungineer* uses psychology and game theory to create social environments, typically digital and mediated, that are layered with choice problems through which the members of the society experience ongoing pleasurable sensations derived from survival-relevant but safe coactivation of motivational systems.

Or, in brief, fungineers create social environments where people have fun. Fungineers are the applied guys; the ivory-tower types in this science would be known as *hedonic game theorists*. They use psychology and game theory to explore the theoretical connections between society, choice, and happiness.

The ideas that fungineers come up with are called *fun policy:* the rules and regulations created by fungineers so as to institute social order. Fun policy theorists would be hedonic game theorists who think conceptually about the design of social orders whose purpose is to provide fun.

It's much easier to imagine this new field of fun policy than to work in it; it does not have many scientists at the moment. All of its theorists are largely practitioners, people who work for game companies. Virtual-world designers with academic positions are a rarity. There are no universities offering Ph.D. degrees in fun policy, though there are many offering master's degrees in game design.

But never mind the absence of fun policy scientists for now; just consider the following argument: If there were such a field as fun policy, its findings could at least be translated into terms that the real world would understand. Both fun policy and real-world policy deal with large numbers of otherwise unassociated people with conflicting interests and desires. Where real-world policy in general ostensibly seeks some kind of aggregate goal (growth in the GDP, for example), fun policy is more explicit: It seeks to allow all of these people to have fun. The goals are different, but the design process is the same. How do you come up with rules and institutions that allow this society of people to reach the goals you believe it wants to achieve? How do you deal with diversity, inequality, and change? How do you discover what people want? How do you know what to implement and when? What affects whether these people generally agree with what you are doing and try to help it along, or oppose it and sabotage your efforts? Such questions are faced with equal intensity by real-world policymakers and by virtual-world designers.

Plenty of able (and brilliant) fun policy practitioners have tried their hand at summarizing concepts of good fun policy design, and because of their efforts a great deal is already known about how one designs a massive and massively fun social environment. These design norms look very much like a handbook of public policy. Such a book would have a structure— chapter and subject headings—that would be familiar to a senior legislative assistant or the head of a government affairs think tank. What knowledge has emerged within the area of practical virtual-world design?

A BUILDING-BY-BUILDING TOUR OF THE SYNTHETIC GOVERNMENT

Virtual-world design practices break down nicely into different areas along the same lines that real-world governments break down their tasks and duties. There are internal affairs, cultural affairs, affairs of war, social affairs, and so on. I will take us on a walk through virtual-world government ministries. In each building, I will describe what game designers and fun policy experts generally do in that area of competence. The focus will be on the standard practices that game designers have determined work very well for the thorny problems of fun policy design. As we tour the practices and policies that have been developed, contrasts and comparisons to real-world governments will become apparent.

Ministry of Constitutional Affairs

Our tour begins with the ministry responsible for the process of policy-making. The creation of new aspects of the social order is handled by the Ministry of Constitutional Affairs. The constitutional arm of the government handles all issues related to the development and execution of policy, law, and regulation.

It is widely understood in the game industry in general, and in virtual-world design in particular, that the right way to design new policies is:

- minimize what the game attempts to do, then
- polish
- polish
- polish

The very best game designs involve the player in a minimally conceived and exquisitely polished set of game mechanics. Common wisdom insists it is far better to have a single core game mechanic that works exceedingly well than to have a large number of different game mechanics that all work fairly well. The industry is filled from top to bottom with creative individuals who are eager to propose and execute new ideas for structuring human interactions, but developers must constantly fight the temptation to add more features to their games. This is known as "feature creep" and is considered a game killer in the industry.

Once basic systems are in place, designers put a great deal of work into systems coordination. Designer Richard Bartle has written extensively about the need to make sure that, say, the operations of the economy do not distort an effort at player self-government.[1] Suppose, for example, that the economic design enabled a small group of players to dominate every critical resource. A player democracy would not emerge under that circumstance.

In addition, no virtual world comes to market without extensive exposure to play testing. This is the core quality assurance method: Get actual people to try out the game before it goes into effect. Then, refine the game and polish. This is why good games can take five years to develop—every detail must be tested, every player experience plumbed.

Even after developers launch a world, feedback from current players is constantly solicited and considered. Open forums solicit comments from players and play testers; employees keep an eye on them. Moreover, everyone understands that the set of rules and policies will change. When players find bugs, problems, and wrong-headed policies, developers make corrections and then they patch the world by issuing a new set of rules. Patches are widely announced beforehand and players are given a preview of policy changes that are about to hit. A test server is maintained where any player can experience the upcoming changes firsthand.

On the whole, the norm of policy creation is to minimize the tasks of government but execute them perfectly in partnership with the players. When Galadail the enchantress is suddenly and unfairly attacked by Jivers, the rogue in the town square, Emily, her owner, can complain loudly on the forums that rogues are somehow able to break the peace in the middle of town. Developers scanning the forums see her complaint, which, if it is valid, is undoubtedly buried in a flood of similar complaints from the thousands and thousands of people who have recently found themselves being attacked by nasty rogues under circumstances that they deem unfair. The "devs" develop a modification of the rules that prevents rogues from making attacks in town. But when they test it out on the test server, they find that their first version of the rule made rogues into helpless victims; because they could not attack in town, others could attack them without risk. Back to the drawing board. The final rule prevents anyone from attacking anyone in the town, thus preserving the peace. The devs patch the new rule onto the world. Those nasty rogues now find the world slightly less fun—no more easy pickings in town—but Galadail and her thousands of fellow victims find the world much more fun now that at least the town is safe. The anger on the forums dissipates, and the devs turn to other problems. Incrementally, a set of rules for common fun emerges.

Ministry of the Interior

Next we come to the ministry in charge of internal affairs. Ministry of the Interior handles all relations between the developer-kings and their citizens. It includes the forums mentioned above, although control over content on the forums is maintained by the Ministry of Justice, below. The Ministry of the Interior appoints class leads whose job is to collect information from players about the performance of the various job classes (i.e., wizard, warrior, etc.). The interior ministry deploys armies of government officials to assist players in their use of the world ("customer service representatives").

Recently, the interior ministry has made a major push toward ease of use. Where at one time new users were simply dropped into the worlds and expected to figure things out on their own, most virtual worlds now have extensive tutorial systems. Moreover, the various features of the world and its government are gradually introduced at a pace dictated by the user. Users increasingly have the option of letting the game systems auto-manage trivial aspects of play. For example, a user may begin to collect herbs and then find his backpacks overflowing with them. Bother! At some level of game mastery, he would discover that he can purchase an "herb bag" that automatically sorts his herbs for him. Convenient!

Finally, Ministry of the Interior officials are moving more and more in the direction of user customization of the entire game experience. *World of Warcraft*'s interface is customizable by the user to a truly exten-

sive degree, and a tiny industry of user interface modification makers
has emerged.

The ministry also maintains a smaller but expanding space dedicated to worlds like *Second Life,* where user-created content is king. Indeed it is somewhat misleading to think of Linden Lab, the company
than runs *Second Life,* as a government. While Linden does have police
power, the company's most powerful role is as the largest land owner.
The jury is still out on whether this content will come to dominate the
ministry in the future.

While we are here in the interior ministry, we should stop in at the
Institute of Mental Health. This annex was built in honor of "Lum the
Mad," the online persona of one Scott Jennings.[2] Jennings played Lum in
the game *Ultima Online (UO)* in the late 1990s and founded a website of
discussion and criticism about the game. Over time, the Lum the Mad
site became one of the most influential locations for reading and learning about the analysis and critique of virtual-world design. Jennings
managed to keep the site both insightful and humorous, and free of the
ranting and immaturity often associated with open-access Internet discussions (especially involving games). Lum's madness, I surmise, had
much to do with Jennings' frustration over the policy decisions of the
owners of *UO.* Lum became a shadow government of sorts, a source of
alternative thinking about what the *UO* government should do. As such,
Lum is the most prominent early example of a substantive government-
citizen dialogue involving virtual worlds. Having observed the emergence of *UO*'s not-always-friendly criticism site, other game developers
have since chosen to provide their own forum and discussion sites. That
way they can directly observe the most heated issues affecting the citizenry, and also quench—by directly censoring posts—any discussion

that becomes too uncomfortable. The evolution of player discussion from an independent voice into a government-owned mouthpiece can only have driven Lum all the more mad, which is why he remains here in the sanitarium.

Ministry of Culture

Let's continue our tour of virtual-world government with the Ministry of Culture, responsible for the creation and maintenance of the lore of the world. The lore is critical for explaining why the activities in the world matter. Few players actively seek the lore, however. Rather, they seep it up through the atmosphere. It is in the air, both unnoticeable and unavoidable at the same time. The brief dialogs that send players on quests are grounded in the lore; the place and creature names come from the lore; even the look and feel of the buildings and landscapes derive from the lore.

Within the lore is the setting of myth, the elements of the backstory that outline the difference between good outcomes and bad ones. Myth is central to the individual player's sense of meaning; it explains why it is important that the player do what he is doing. A well-written myth makes the game's structures deeply and apparently survival relevant, which is integral to the intensification of fun. A good myth must be deep, not trivial. At the same time, it must not be too serious for the real lives of the players, otherwise the sense of play is lost. Tolkien's Middle Earth myth paints a generic war of good versus evil, and has been a popular (though often indirect) source of lore. Lewis' Narnia would not work as well, because the analogs to Christianity are too apparent. Blasphemy against Aslan in the game world would be awfully close to real blasphemy against the Lord. For some, Narnia might be a good, fun world; for others, it would be a fun world for all the wrong reasons. And those two groups would not mix well.

This leads to a final duty of the culture ministry, which is to maintain an aesthetic consistency across the various elements of the world. Sound and visuals must match with quests and player capabilities in one organic whole. A world about the peaceful exploration of nature will not have bulldozers and chainsaws in it—unless environmental policy conflict is part of the vision.

Ministry of War

The Ministry of War handles all the fighting. The core role of the combat system of a virtual world is to induce intense coactivation, which of course is integral to the generation of fun. Combat provides the aversive element of coactivation because it introduces a failure state, labeled *death*. Usually when a character "dies," she is transported involuntarily to a distant site, sometimes with some penalty in terms of damaged equipment or loss of money or "experience points." The character is delayed, turned away, frustrated—but never defeated. A dogged player will come back again and again until the challenge that led to death is overcome. The game is designed so that the challenge will always remain there, waiting.

Allowing fighting in groups of five to ten players is an effective coactivation tool: On the positive side, the player receives the rewards of sociality, as well as a share of treasure. On the negative side, there is nothing like a large group of combatants for attracting the attention of large groups of enemies. As strong as coactivation might be from groups, it is stronger still from raids, which are squads of 20 to 200 players. The association of raid groups with realms, which makes the raid group effectively an army, further intensifies coactivation.

The combat system is the location of power over the world, the basic system whereby the player is able to secure resources, travel, and acquire reputation. Power is measured primarily in the form of experience points. The more you have, the more powerful you are. You get experience points by completing jobs in the world, that is, by defeating the challenges the world presents. Most of the time, the completion of jobs requires that you defeat monsters. It's a recipe for coactivation in a metaphorical structure that could not get closer to the task of survival: Kill the threat and take the resource that helps overcome such threats more handily in the future.

It is not necessary to use combat as the road to power, but it is nonetheless the norm. Physical combat predominates because it is obviously relevant to survival. Early hominids made themselves safe by beating, slashing, and spearing their enemies. For evolutionary reasons, violence, conflict, risk, danger, and warfare provide high levels of situational intensity, energizing the emotions. You could design a world in which all the players climb small hills and pick flowers at the top, with each flower adding to their flower collection. Or you could place the flowers at the bottom of a long, complex dungeon, guarded by fearsome monsters and demons, and make the flowers powerful, so that once you pick one you can throw it at the demons and destroy them. Both games have goals and challenges, but the second is just more exciting. It pumps more zing into the motivational system, producing more intense emotions.

With fighting being the usual road to power, the combat system is where the most power balancing needs to be done. Different players have different styles and abilities, and they all have to have a fair shot at combat efficacy. Usually this is done by allowing players to choose from among a limited set of combat classes: rogues, wizards, warriors, clerics. These classes all go about their fighting in different ways, and each way has to be about equally successful. If any one of them becomes more powerful than the others, many players will choose that class over the others. The expectation in the war ministry is that any player can choose any class, and have a reasonable expectation of being roughly as powerful as any other player. Meeting this expectation is a gargantuan design task, yet largely achieved. Success is attained here through careful attention to the standards of the Ministry of Constitutional Affairs: minimize features and then polish, polish, polish before finally imposing the policy.

Another tool of power balancing is leveling, a system that awards any player with new power once he or she achieves certain objectives. It may take different players different amounts of time to achieve these objectives, but the objectives are designed so that any player can reach them eventually. Once a player meets the objectives, she receives the powers. With these powers, the player is now capable of defeating or otherwise outclassing all players at lower levels. The system ignores how long it took the player to get to that level. Such leveling systems mute the effects of the distribution of player skill.

The analog in the real world would be the following. Suppose Harvard had an admissions policy based on a standardized test, and the rules were that once someone accumulated 10,000 test points, she was admitted. The test is given once a year and has 1,000 new questions each year, each worth 10 points. Some people will do the test perfectly at the first try, and will be immediately admitted. Others will take two or three years to accumulate 10,000 points. Still others may take decades. However, virtually anyone can eventually be admitted to Harvard. Moreover, every admitted person receives all of the rewards and privileges that attend admission, regardless of how long it took her to get in. Indeed, once admitted, students may apply to Harvard Law School using the same system—accumulate 10,000 points on the Harvard Law School exam, and advance to the next level.

Such leveling systems serve multiple purposes. They make it possible for the world to have both success and fairness. Success is measured by advancement in power, and it is possible for anyone to advance. There are no glass ceilings in virtual worlds. The top jobs—the highest levels of power—are not conceived as singular positions of authority, but rather as common layers of nobility. Within these layers, players still maintain reputational hierarchies and informally coronate one another as the "best" level 60 fire wizard. But this is not recognized by the system. All fire wizards can become level 60 fire wizards, and when they do, their fireballs will be just as devastating to level 20 warriors as those of any other level 60 fire wizard. "Leveling" thus accurately defines the functions of the system, which is to level power across people, ensuring that balance is maintained.

A final service performed by combat and leveling is dynamic challenge adjustment. In order to sustain coactivation and have a hope of sustaining flow, the game system must get harder when the player gets better. The experience points system has this automatic effect: The more times you defeat a monster of a certain type and challenge level, the more points you accumulate, and the more points you have, the easier it is to defeat that monster. When boredom is reached, move on to a tougher monster, who indeed offers more points. Rinse and repeat. The flow of challenge-optimized confrontations is nearly endless and systems have been designed that can keep a player motivated for hours and hours.

Related to dynamic challenge adjustment is the task of pattern shifting. It is necessary to vary the game experience quickly once it is evident that the player has "pattern-matched": become consciously or uncon-sciously aware of the next thing the system is about to throw at him. Since the combat system is the location of most challenge, risk, and threat, the combat system is where variations in the challenge level must happen. Leveling helps achieve this. Players who have reached higher levels can be assumed to have mastered the basic play modes of the first levels, and can be subjected to new ones. Beyond this, the system can keep track of the player's success with respect to various challenges and begin to tilt the playing field somewhat in the player's favor if progress is slow. Many worlds now allow for a catch-up mode: Players who take a break from the game—possibly because of frustration—gain power and treasure more quickly for a period after their return.

In all, the Ministry of War occupies a central position, providing the core mechanics of fun generation.

Ministry of Economics

Next we come to the ministry in charge of commerce. Markets, it turns out, have long since been known to be an important source of fun in these societies. For example, the synthetic world *EverQuest (EQ)* has been described as a "gear game": Your character's power depends almost en-tirely on the items she possesses. She gets some of these items directly, by taking them from monsters, but she gets many of them simply by buying them in markets. *EQ* and most games since have had dramatically active player-to-player markets—with gear being so important, players have to sell gear they can't use so they can buy gear that they can use. Crowds of players often stand around in virtual marketplaces—which can spring up anywhere, from towns to tunnels to forests—hawking their wares like merchants of old.

The economic system serves as a parallel to the combat system in the coactivation of player motivation; where combat activates the aversive system, treasure and loot activates the appetitive system. Whenever a player does anything that is remotely successful—even killing the smallest mouse if it stands in the way—the player receives a bit of treasure. Maybe it is only a few copper pieces, but it is instant gratification. Players who engage a stream of enemies thereby receive a more or less constant stream of small economic and power rewards (along with experience points that raise their combat level), which contributes to the sense of flow.

The Ministry of Economics is responsible for ensuring zero unemployment. It is considered absolutely intolerable that a player have nothing to do. Quests are, in effect, ad hoc job contracts: The nonplayer character says "Go do this task for me, and I will pay you something for it." The system ensures that there is always another quest to do. If there are no quests, players may on their own initiative go into the world and harvest resources. Sometimes this is a peaceful task: One simply looks for iron ore chunks or thistledown blooms and gathers them up. Other times combat is involved—monsters must be shooed away, or the monsters are carrying the resources needed. The wolf does not voluntarily give up his pelt. Harvested resources always have a demand price—nonplayer merchants are always standing by, willing to buy the harvested goods even if no players are interested. In a sound economic system, the demand comes from players, but again it is intolerable that there be no positive demand whatsoever for a player's work output. Thus the system must guarantee that every player, at all times, has something productive to do, some way of turning his own action into some reward.

It is also intolerable that any player begin the game with an economic advantage. Rather, every new character is born into the world quite literally with his shirt on his back and perhaps a rusty sword or an old club. Nothing more. Though not all will become equally rich, all must start out equally poor. The Ministry of Economics opposes any system of inheritance except between characters owned by the same person. To transfer massive amounts of resources from a successful first character to a second newborn character is called *twinking* and is accepted by the ministry. It is a way for players to experience a new type of character while moving through content at a more rapid pace; consistent with dynamic challenge adjustment, the player does not get quite as bored with this already-seen content because his more-powerful character moves through it more quickly. Other than this, though, the Ministry of Economics insists that the starting line be the same for all players.

Resources are endowed with positive market demand by extensive crafting systems. Crafting is production, designed so that its optimal organization is preindustrial. There are no factories in virtual worlds. There is plenty of rote work, but it is self-managed and self-motivated. Crafters are generally designed to be lonely artisans who spend countless hours perfecting their characters' skill levels. When the highest skill levels are attained, the crafter becomes one of the few capable of making certain desired objects. In order to reach such levels, crafters need to practice by creating large numbers of less valuable items, items that they simply throw away. In making those items, however, these crafters-in-training create demand for the resources out in the world. These are in turn harvested by other players, the more adventuresome types, who relish the idea, for example, of facing dangers in order to acquire a certain ore that has a high price in the market. Leveling in crafting systems follows the same norms as in combat: Anyone can attain the highest level; once they do, all powers and rights and abilities associated with that level are granted, and the speed of advance is forgotten.

As with combat, crafting jobs must be balanced. It cannot be tolerated that jewelcrafters advance to the highest skill levels more quickly than leatherworkers. Nor can it be more fun or lucrative to be a tailor than a chef. Jobs must be balanced. Moreover, the crafting system must exhibit specialization: Tailors must need pins from metalworkers, who need ore from miners, who need wood from loggers, who need shipping from sailors, who need boats from shipwrights, who need sails from tailors. Even the loot gained from monsters is specialized: A warrior who obtains a wonderful magic wand from an evil sorcerer has no use for it herself; she will therefore sell it to other players on the player market. Specialization creates gains from trade and helps attain the zero unemployment norm.

The approach to markets is unabashedly positive. Markets are considered very important. The absolute minimum transaction cost is sought. Currency is lightweight, convenient, and maintains something of a stable value (but not perfectly stable). During purchases, change is automatically made and coins are automatically sorted into the coin purse. Anyone is able to obtain more currency at any time through simple rote activities, such as hunting lower-level, lower-risk monsters for their lower-level treasures. The economics ministry does not tolerate the exclusion of any person from full and complete participation in the economy.

Under longstanding economics ministry policy, there are no taxes. For all intents and purposes, government obtains revenue and resources through magic: It creates them out of thin air. It is indeed a singular power of virtual-world governments that they can create anything for free, except labor. In some cases, governments have learned that it is sensible to apply usage fees to control demand and prevent overburdening the infrastructure. Fees are usually applied to storage and transportation systems, as well as market transactions.

Ministry of Social Affairs

Continuing on our tour, we come to a building dedicated to social interactions among the players, which are often notably deep. The world of *Star Wars Galaxies* was at times filled with dancers, musicians, chefs, doctors, make-up artists, and clothing designers, even politicians. I once visited a town meeting there, which had the Rockwellian feel of any town meeting—except that some of the citizens had fur all over their bodies or horns on their heads or looked like big squids. Otherwise, it was a perfectly acceptable emulation of Dixville Notch.

The social affairs ministry focuses on policies that enable players to form into groups. It works with the war ministry in the construction of combat groups, raid groups, and armies. But the main focus is on social organizations, primarily known as guilds. Guild management is enabled and simplified through the interface. Usually a player needs to bring together a group of ten or so colleagues to found the guild. Thereafter, new members can be invited to join, and the organization can grow to almost any size. Guild structures bring many advantages in the creation of fun. Foremost, they solidify the sense of meaning and significance in the win and loss states (treasure and death), validating players' emotional sensibilities about them. Within the context of a tightly cohesive guild, it is anathema to proclaim that treasure is not important or death is a trivial event. Many guilds aspire to military cohesion, with members expected to contribute many hours every night to raids. The greatest rewards in the game are protected by the most fearsome, powerful, and crafty opponents, and it takes a highly coordinated raid to best them. Elite guilds are the only ones able to deploy such coordinated forces, meaning that, in effect, the end-game content incents the player base to found such guilds and work toward making them a reality.

The Ministry of Social Affairs feels that all players should be encouraged in one way or another to be a member of some kind of group or guild. It encourages designs that withhold key rewards in such a way that players must form some kind of a group to win them. It also promotes combat and crafting system designs that force teamwork; the most powerful combat group should have a mix of combat types in it, so that everyone matters regardless of the type of character they like to play.

The ministry's efforts to get people working together capitalize on its understanding of the importance of human networks as a source of human satisfaction and sense of belonging. If everyone has something to contribute to groups, and if groups are always in need of more members, it becomes the norm for individuals to step out of their isolation and pitch in. And they are always welcomed. This makes everyone feel needed. It also makes the job of the Ministry of Justice a bit easier, since groups can stigmatize players who misbehave. Through network effects, the world also better retains the allegiance of its members. They may no longer care about the game's content, but they do care about the feelings of the friends they have made, so they remain committed to making this world a better place.

The social affairs ministry enables these grouping structures primarily through social organization interface tools, as mentioned above, but also through the privileged communications. Guild members share their own private chat channel. But beyond this, chat channels are manipulated and deployed to bring people together. Players can be automatically added to a region-wide chat channel, to a level-restricted chat channel, or to a raid-restricted chat channel. As virtual worlds gradually adopt internet telephony, these protocols will be applied to voice communications.

As the ministry concerned most with the community aspects of virtual-world societies, the social affairs ministry regulates policy concerning the public use of wealth and power. It insists that players have the ability to show off their wealth and achievements. Conspicuous consumption is to be encouraged. The most powerful swords are therefore the largest, the brightest, the flashiest. The high-level priest's robes must dazzle like the sun itself. By comparison, the rags of the newborn need only protect modesty; indeed, they ought to be rather ugly.

Parallel to conspicuous consumption is a general norm against charity. All players start with nothing and are expected to make their own way forward. More powerful characters may help with a coin or two, or with guidance through the tough spots of a terrible dungeon, but the general expectation is that each player acquires power and resources through her own efforts. Charity douses the aversive activation system, making the game boring. By frowning on charity, the ministry reminds players that there is a difference between wants and likes. Every player wants to advance more quickly through the game, but if that wish is granted, the player will not like the result. If a player could advance immediately to the highest level and obtain every treasure and reward in the system with the click of a button, only one motivation system would be activated and boredom will result. No flow. The aversive system activators must be defended at all costs, even at the cost of discouraging help from friends.

Ministry of Justice

Finally, we come to the Ministry of Justice. The need for law enforcement is illustrated by stories from the early days of the world of *Ultima Online*, when it became apparent that a certain number of players were in the world primarily because they wanted to harass other players. At the time, the developers felt that such behavior should simply be tolerated, that any attempt to crack down on this harassment would just turn the entire player base against the game's owners. One of those developers, Gordon Walton, felt otherwise. Having carried the handle "Tyrant" for many years in the online game industry, he argued from within *UO*'s administration that anti-harassment provisions in the terms of service ought to be enforced strenuously. Walton argued that since most players were in the game just to have a good time, enforcement against harassing elements would be welcomed. In this spirit, Walton intervened in the community with an iron fist, aggressively banning players who violated the terms of service. Most observers now agree that synthetic world governments simply must enforce some level of behavioral law in order to keep their games reasonably enjoyable.

Therefore, the Ministry of Justice is proud of its longstanding tradition of tyranny with respect to the rules. Cheating is absolutely forbidden. Cheating is defined as any action that contravenes the terms of service, to which all players agree when they enter the game world. For the most part, the penalty for cheating is summary execution. Characters can't be shot on the spot (players still less so), but "execution" occurs nonetheless, in the form of suspension and banning of accounts. It is a severe penalty. A character may have amassed thousands of real dollars worth of resources and powers. It could represent the accumulation of thousands of hours of time. To ban the account is to destroy all the wealth along with the character.

The ministry also pooh-poohs any calls for proper procedure. There is no due process. Agents of the ministry, called "GMs" for "game-masters," are summoned to a conflict or notified of a rules violation by players. The GM weighs options and takes testimony in what is little more than a drumhead trial. He may confer with other employees of the ministry. A ruling is issued. There are appeals, but the courts to which they must be directed are Kafkaesque. It is a legal system that stresses speed and efficiency, not necessarily justice—for better or for worse.

The laws administered by the Ministry of Justice forbid such things as "exploits," tricking monsters into easy deaths; "AFK macroing," using a computer program to play; and "dupes," exploiting bugs in the system to autogenerate massive amounts of wealth. Harassment of other players, verbally or through combat actions, is also forbidden.

The Ministry of Justice does not try to enforce every rule in its very lengthy rulebook. One strategy it encourages is to split the player base according to variations in the players' sense of law. For example, some players enjoy harassing one another through direct combat between characters of unequal level, a ruleset known as "open-level player-vs-player" (or PVP). That is, some players feel it is fun game play for level 60 characters to be able to attack and kill level 10 characters over and over. Typically, the players who enjoy this are the ones who get to level 60 the quickest. On the face of it, of course, the brutality of such an environment is apparent. Violence in games may or may not be deplorable, but rule sets that encourage and reward bullying are clearly nothing to be proud of. Some players hate this sort of thing. If players who hate it and players who love it are thrown together, the conflicts that result (about fairness, equality, safety, etc.) are incredibly difficult to police in a way that keeps everyone happy. Therefore the ministry encourages the designation of different rules for different servers: In one version of the world, open-level PVP is considered okay and will not be subject to sanction. In other worlds, PVP is not allowed, and is directly prevented through code. Those who love or hate open-level PVP can sort themselves accordingly, saving the ministry from much work.

A similar split-population approach saves the Ministry of Justice from worrying too much about economic policy violations. The economics ministry prefers strongly that every player start with zero resources, yet some players use external markets to trade dollars for gold pieces. Their characters thus enter the world as wealthy but inexperienced. The Ministry of Justice generally turns a blind eye here, since the external markets are beyond its jurisdiction. In the virtual world, the exchange just looks like charity—character A gives character B 10,000 gold pieces for nothing. No rule appears to be broken. Yet since this activity violates a strongly held policy of one of the more powerful ministries, something ought to be done. One answer is to systematically make it impossible for massive amounts of wealth to yield huge increases in the advancement pace. If gear is rated as being only usable by a character of level 20, a level 1 character cannot use it, no matter how powerful it is and no matter how much money he may have. But another approach is to open entire servers where real-money trading is approved, in the hopes that, as with PVP servers, these servers will draw the most noxious behavior to them.

END OF TOUR

These policies and procedures have now become standard in virtual worlds and constitute a veritable handbook of human motivation: "How to Get Someone to Play in Your World for Thousands and Thousands of

Hours." The same book could be retitled "How to Build a Fun Society: Practical Rules for Government." This wisdom has been built up gradually, through trial and error, but the results are impressive. These policies work. It is indeed remarkable: Game designers have been given a set of human beings with the same motivations as the citizens of real-world governments, and have designed for these people a set of social structures that allows just about everybody to have fun all the time. Who knew that so many people could enjoy so much time together? Amazing. Yet real people are indeed putting thousands and thousands of hours into worlds built on these principles. If there is a science of fun policy, this is it. Once people are exposed to this science, and soon hundreds of millions of people will be, will they clamor for fun policy in the real world?

PART THREE

HOW THE EXODUS AFFECTS THE REAL WORLD

CHAPTER EIGHT

THE FUN ECONOMY

The rules that virtual-world designers lay down—their public policy—will affect policies in the real world. Throughout history, whenever people have moved from one country to another—from Austria to Hungary or vice versa—policies are compared. Voter interests are exchanged. If Hungarians are enjoying a policy that makes sense and would be popular in Austria, Austrians hear about it from their departed relatives and friends, and then press their government for that policy. When people move from the real world to the virtual world, they will assess the policies encountered in the virtual world and then ask why things are different in the real world. If the people who play in virtual worlds truly enjoy the economic, political, and social games they are being offered there, it makes sense that they would become a force for change in the real world. The policy pressure on the real world will get more intense as the number of virtual-world players rises from dozens of millions to hundreds of millions. All of these gamers will bring an awareness of alternative policies into the real world. At first, it won't matter whether those policies have any realistic possibility of implementation. They will simply be what the gamers expect. It is no great stretch to predict that these policy preferences, which people *develop* in virtual worlds, will eventually be *expressed* in the real world. It is a change mechanism that delivers credible, and very sobering, food for thought.

What will happen when "the way things are" in synthetic worlds becomes compared, almost unconsciously, to "the way things are" in the real world? Citizens will express increasing dissatisfaction with real-world governments. Real-world governments must respond by either providing good reasons for the difference in the worlds, or by amending policy accordingly. The former response will be the only answer available in many cases, of course, since we cannot snap our fingers and conform the real world to a virtual world. Yet in many cases, the latter response is necessary, and real-world policies will change accordingly. As such, virtual worlds are policy laboratories, placing real-world humans in radically different policy environments. These virtual-world policies do not have traditional targets—income, wealth, and so on—but rather the production of the longest possible sequence of continuously fun activities. An application of the principles of fun policy in the real world would represent radical change, a fun revolution. Change is always traumatic. But the payoff from implementing what the game designers have learned is a significant increase in human happiness. There are some good reasons why an increase of fun in the real world could be problematic, and I will discuss those soon. But at first blush, we have to ask, Why not? Why not make the game of the real world more fun for everyone?

Of course, much of what goes on in synthetic worlds is never going to be relevant for the real world. The real world will never be able to make invisible spaceships available to anyone, so a synthetic world's experience at providing invisible spaceships is not going to provide much advice about doing the same in the real world. The topics I've selected for discussion are strictly those where I think it is feasible for the policies of the virtual world to become policies in the real world. Because not all policy transfers are equally feasible or likely, I have arranged the topics in order of their likelihood of transfer. That is, you should think of the items on the top of the list as ones where significant pressure for change will happen. They are considered central to the creation of fun, and no one would even consider making a fun social order without them. Virtual-world citizens will find it increasingly appalling that the real world does not work this way. Thus as the real world faces pressure to become more fun, reforms are most likely to be applied at the top of this list. The items near the bottom are not as integral to the creation of fun. Even though we may end up living in a society dedicated to fun, pressure to reform in these directions will not be as strong.

The topics are:

- employment and unemployment
- equality of opportunity
- equality of outcomes
- social insurance and the welfare state
- wages and corporate structure
- economic growth
- taxation
- inflation and monetary policy

EMPLOYMENT AND UNEMPLOYMENT

The strongest and at the same time most radical economic prescription of virtual-world design is *full employment*. Every person who wants work *must* have work, at all times. It is not of tremendous significance that the work be well paid; what matters is that the work be meaningful. It must help the world somehow and earn the worker some small amount of money or power. To follow this prescription, real-world governments will have to make minimum-wage jobs available to anyone who wants them. Even if they are of a make-work character, they must be obviously directed toward accomplishing something. Of course, the very notion of government-supplied work for all evokes an era and a collection of socialistic philosophies now discredited both in theory and in the execution of human history. But it only evokes; it does not revitalize. Full employment is not being advocated here as a sacred mission of a justice-seeking all-powerful State. Rather, it is just a newly discovered tool that helps make the game of life fun for everybody.

When I visited the Soviet Union as a youth, I remember seeing old ladies sitting around in the few stores open to Westerners. They did nothing, basically. It was their job to do nothing. They sat there all day, bored and unhappy, and received a few rubles for their trouble. The dream of universal employment had been realized, but in a completely dehumanizing way.

Contrast that to a typical experience in *EverQuest*. You walk through the streets and fields and run across nonplayer characters with quills floating above their heads. Click on the Farmer Walcott and he starts to talk to you, telling you of the problems he has keeping insects out of his field. He asks you to kill the insects. It takes you some time, and you get a few silver pieces. You haven't saved the world, but you did something that mattered a little, and you got a little coin for it. As soon as you finish with Farmer Walcott, you run into Captain Eitoa of the City Guard. She asks you to go on an exploration mission. And so on, ad infinitum; consistent with the name *EverQuest,* which is to say you are always on a mission, always have something to do, and are always seeking.

Gamer generations will not only expect work to be universally available, but also organized as *self-employment with voluntary yet profitable team building.* Virtual-world workers control their own economic lives. They do work with others, indeed that is part of the fun. But the teams are built voluntarily. Every team member wants to be in the team, and everyone on the team is glad that the team has that member. When the team's work finishes, each worker takes his share of rewards and puts them toward his own affairs as he sees fit. All organization is ad hoc and voluntary. Success is leveraged into networks and reputation, which become keys to being invited to better teams. The organizational structure of production in today's games is utterly flat, with no bosses except yourself. Yet, a need for teamwork has been introduced into the production function. As these forms of organization become more common, it will become normal for workers in the real world to step beyond their isolation and voluntarily commune together.

EQUALITY OF OPPORTUNITY

The second strongest norm in fun policy design, and one equally radical, is that of *equality of opportunity.* In any game, all players start on an equal basis. Otherwise the game is not fair. Games that are not fair are not fun. The economic game of the real world thus will face pressure to become more fair if it is to respond adequately to the exodus to virtual worlds.

The norm in virtual worlds is that every person starts in abject poverty. In the space game *Eve Online,* a new player gets a thin-hulled little ship that can be easily blasted to bits by all the other players. Every new player must scavenge and scrape to work himself up to a ship that can defend itself or run away. Tough, but fair: Everybody starts out with zero wealth. In the real world, this would imply an estate tax of greater than 100 percent—not only would all inheritances be forbidden, but whatever resources a child might be born with would have to be taken away as well. This would be madness, of course; the virtual world can start all players at $0 income because they don't need to eat to survive. Although, since work is always available, anyone who needs money to (virtually) "eat" can get it.

However, pressure to equalize the starting line in life will become significant. It has often been proposed before that equality of opportunity ought to the guiding principle of social policy.[1] The effect of virtual worlds may be to increase public support for these ideas. In concrete terms, it may become popular to tax things like bequests, which confer starting-line advantages on those who are already ahead, and transfer the proceeds to things like low-income education, so as to confer starting-line advantages on those who are already behind. Policymakers may come to realize that significant social problems in countries with as much inequality as the United States do not come from income disparities per se but from perceptions that the economic game is not fair. Policies that make the economic game obviously fairer are likely to become more popular as virtual worlds broaden their influence.

EQUALITY OF OUTCOMES

While virtual-world citizens value equality of opportunity, the same cannot be said of equality of outcomes. Perhaps more than any other issue, the gap between rich and poor has dominated social thinking for hundreds of years. Communism, with its ideology of economic equality, defined history and politics for generations, while in America, the welfare state attempts to banish inequality.

All the same, funny things are happening online that make one wonder whether we are truly satisfied with this struggle. Online games exhibit economic inequality so vast and so obvious that it dwarfs real-world inequality. When warriors acquire their priceless, epic, two-handed sword— usually a massive, glowing, singing pillar of shiny red steel that they carry around everywhere they go—they *flaunt* it. In Blizzard Entertainment's *World of Warcraft*, the most successful members of the paladin class have suits of armor with a dazzle-factor that is truly difficult to convey. Richly polished helms that shine like the very sun. Shoulder armor that rises up around the wearer's head like a glittering golden corona. Majestic horses adorned in jewels and rich fabrics. It's showy enough to be almost silly. Yet it is de rigueur: If you've got material wealth, you are expected to wave it around in everyone's face. That in itself may not seem very strange, of course; humans are showy as peacocks at times.

What's strange is the fact that nobody seems to care. There's envy, yes, but nothing that needs to be addressed as a policy matter. It should be noted that policy discussions are an integral part of the community of these games. Most virtual-world owners maintain public online forums where players can air grievances, make suggestions, ask for help, or just discuss game events. Through these forums an outside observer can see what sorts of issues motivate the players to make policy suggestions or criticisms. This is all couched in the terms of game design, of course; the designers do not think of themselves as a government, and the players don't think of themselves as citizens.

But any public policy expert would recognize these debates for what they are: Efforts by a citizenry to persuade its government to change the rules. And what is striking is that one simply never sees a call for more "vertical equity," a term used by income analysts to refer to equality between people in different stations in life. For example, vertical equity demands that CEOs, who get paid more, should pay higher taxes than mailroom workers. In the real world, vertical equity concerns motivate considerable discussion, anger, and debate. Not in the virtual world. In the virtual world, everyone thinks that the more powerful and wealthy a character becomes, the greater the available rewards should be. Why? Because that's the very nature of fun. When a poor man has a chance to win $100, he is very excited. When a rich man has the same chance, he is bored. Thus from the standpoint of fun, richer people should have the chance to win bigger prizes.

Game designs reflect this principle to the nth degree. The moment one acquires some new power, one gains access to game content that, when mastered, offers greater rewards: more treasure, more abilities, more prestige. And more power too, of course, which introduces you to yet another level of riches. This process continues until your character enters what is called "the end game" or "the elder game," incredibly fun content designed to be held back only for those players who build the most powerful and wealthy characters. To the wealthy go the greatest spoils, and no one complains.

The players do not complain about a lack of vertical equity, but they howl about failed horizontal equity. Horizontal equity refers to the notion that people in the same life station should bear the same burdens and reap the same rewards. Players have an acute and finely honed sense of who is at what level of power in the game, and how their rewards and burdens differ. Most games have a system of jobs or "classes" that characters can choose from. You might choose to make your character a wizard, or a warrior, or a priest, or a rogue. Depending on that choice, your character will have unique abilities: Warriors use heavy armor, wizards cast spells, priests heal wounds, rogues pick pockets. Woe to the game designer who makes spell-casting more powerful than heavy armor. Warriors will not stand for it. First they will complain. Then they will publicly bad-mouth your game. Then they will leave. Meanwhile, wizards will be happily playing the game, saying nothing to anyone because they are too busy reaping the rewards of privilege. This is an unhappy scenario for the developers, and they avoid it assiduously by "balancing" classes.

Class balancing is considered so important that it has become refined into an art among the game design community. The norm being pursued is almost ridiculously hard when viewed as social policy. First, the agency of the user has to be completely respected: Users expect to be able to choose whatever class they want, and still have just as much fun as the next guy. Second, users expect that their opportunities for fun will be exactly the same as everyone else at their "level," at all times, in all situations, at all levels. What's amazing is that these goals of horizontal equity are largely achieved. There are games with dozens of classes, dozens of player races (elves, dwarves, etc.), dozens of geographical areas, and dozens of levels—a problem space with about 12^4 or 20,736 corners—all of them being roughly balanced horizontally in terms of fun.

It appears that so long as everyone has the same opportunities—guaranteed by the equality of opportunity principle discussed above and class balancing—it is okay if the outcomes are wildly different. Indeed, it is more fun if the outcomes differ. If everyone starts out with nothing, and if no one has any special advantages as play proceeds, and if everyone has the chance to eventually acquire all the goodies so long as they keep playing, then everyone can live out a true Horatio Alger story.

In the real world, as far as social policy is concerned, we have treated Horatio Alger as a fairy tale, and instead worked hard to transfer money to the less fortunate on the assumption that pulling yourself up to vast wealth by your bootstraps is not feasible for most poor people. Virtual-world designers are inheritors of a 30-year role-playing game tradition that treats such bootstrap-pulling as a defining element of what has become an exceedingly successful commercial game design genre. Millions of people pay good money to be Horatio Alger; it is apparently really fun. And in Horatio Alger's world: (A) everyone has a chance to succeed, (B) everyone does succeed, and (C) those succeeding get very rich. And they are not ashamed of wealth either; they flaunt it. This is the content of virtual-world social policy: rags to riches for all.

However, rags to riches represents an earthquake for social policy in the real world. In the real world, the assumption is that poverty is a more or less unavoidable condition for most people; either by bad luck or bad behavior, the poor are just poor and our response should be to give a helping hand. The idea of providing complete horizontal equity is as far from the social policy agenda as having poorhouses on the moon. Meanwhile, in the real world we hate vertical equity: We expect the rich to make donations and be humble, and we have entire markets for goods that make people look rich who aren't, a category of "conspicuous consumption" that truly rich people are expected to avoid.

Like the horizontal/vertical equity arrangements in the virtual world, these real-world arrangements go together. *Because* the starting line is not equal, winning the race is nothing to shout about. *Because* the playing field is not even, touchdowns should be celebrated with some reservation and proper decorum. The fun that rich people have in winning that huge contract or making that killing on the stock market is largely kept secret, a private pleasure. Thus, to move society toward a genuine rags-to-riches policy would mark a truly dramatic shift, an upheaval, in our approach to equity.

Yet the idea of an institutionalized rags-to-riches storyline for the real world is not completely far-fetched. As I have already argued, economists and social policy experts have suggested often in the past that the best answer to poverty is equality of opportunity. That is exactly the sort of social policy that gamers would expect: a level playing field, with freedom to flaunt your wealth.

SOCIAL INSURANCE AND THE WELFARE STATE

There is *no welfare* and *no charity* in virtual worlds. Part of the reason is because of the previous two policies: Jobs are available for all, and those jobs offer anyone a decent chance of advancing. Such policies offer a kind of perpetual insurance against failure. Moreover, the failure state in virtual worlds is labeled "death," but in fact is nothing so severe. It is just a teleportation with a minor time penalty attached. There being no credit, no one becomes bankrupt. Everyone being self-employed, all failures are largely owned by the person who commits them.

Thus, economic life in virtual worlds is not easy. The state makes it possible for anyone to *work* his way forward—there are no handouts of any kind. In this, the government seems awfully indifferent to the economic sufferings of its citizens. But here again is an insight about the nature of fun. Some amount of indifference to economic suffering is integral to having true challenge in the world. Without challenge, there is no fun. Virtual worlds offer a fair start and guaranteed minimum-wage employment. They do not guarantee success, though, and the reason is that the worlds would be no fun at all if they did.

The impact on the real world here would be just as radical as in the previous policy areas, but in a different direction. Removal of welfare state supports is a radically libertarian philosophy. But again, its roots are not in Bentham, Mill, Thatcher, and Reagan. Here, the roots of the idea are in virtual worlds and the practices of virtual-world designers, seeking always to make economic systems in which people seek out activities that they enjoy. Government intervention that just solves someone's problem and removes the challenge may make the person relieved, for awhile anyway, but it is no fun. There's no sense of mastery in it, no sense of achievement, no sense of self-efficacy.

Real-world policies like the Earned Income Tax Credit (EITC) fit here: EITC is a credit that gets applied to a person's wages at tax time, so long as those wages are positive but low. To the worker, the EITC looks like a big tax refund—it does not look like "welfare." We know from many studies that welfare recipients view a dollar of welfare as worth less than a dollar of income. In other words, getting charity stinks. The EITC overcomes this impression, simply by making welfare look like a bigger paycheck. It is an invisible, dynamic, difficulty adjustment system, and game designers would have predicted its general popularity.

From a game design perspective, most social insurance systems make good sense as tools for encouraging fun. The myth that U.S. Social Security simply pays back to a worker funds that were paid in over the course of the work life is effective in the promotion of a sense of joy and fairness in play—so long as the fiction holds. Better would be a policy that truly insured people. That would make the economic game more pleasant by taking some of the sting out of not doing well. A better social safety net lets everyone enjoy themselves on the economic trapeze.

This discussion here treats the economy as play, something that only makes sense (if at all) in a rich country whose citizens can afford to play with the ups and downs of income and wealth. Not all countries are that rich. The economy is not play anywhere that starvation is an issue, because economic loss is dangerous to your health. It's hard to be light-hearted about a competition in which losing might mean starving to death. Because of this, one might be tempted to conclude that the economy cannot be play anywhere at all. But it is important to remember that starvation is not a major issue in large developed countries. In the United States, it has been recognized since the 1950s that the problems of human welfare do not involve mere survival.[2] Our policy problem is not starvation, it is unhappiness. As long as we continue to live in affluence, our social conversation will tend to concern itself with the joy of eating rather than the contribution of food to survival. The emergence of whole societies where the only thing happening is game playing is just more evidence that—for better or for worse—our concerns about human well-being have changed from mere survival to living the right way. Since many people feel that having fun is integral to living the right way, our welfare state will be expected to address the lack of fun in the economy as this century proceeds.

WAGES AND CORPORATE STRUCTURE

Virtual-world designers, if (when!) given the real economy as a design problem, would first suggest universal employment at some minimal wage; they would also suggest a specific wage structure. If their recommendations are accepted, we will see our pay shrink in size but increase in frequency, so that we get little bits of money every time we accomplish

This happened in the game *EverQuest* when I toured it in the late 1990s. It was clear that money was flowing into the world too quickly, and the prices of high-end items were simply skyrocketing. Yet at the same time, oddly, the prices of low-end items, items for poor characters such as mine, were consistently falling. Prices shouldn't fall when the money supply is growing rapidly, so this was puzzling. The explanation was that the money flowing into the world was fairly spread out across levels, but the gear was not. The highest players eagerly sought the very best gear and would pay anything for it. When they obtained it, they sold their old gear to lower-level players, who then sold their old gear to still lower players, and so on down the line. As gear flowed down the levels, money flowed up. This caused rapid inflation at the top, but a decline in prices at the bottom. The net effect was a dramatic increase in real wages for the lower-level players: An hour's worth of earnings would turn into a much better set of gear than it used to. Designer Raph Koster calls this "database inflation"—there's more of everything flowing in. The players are getting richer, top to bottom. There's inflation, but real economic wealth is rising nonetheless. And that is perceived not as a benefit, but a problem. Gradually, the game world is losing its challenge and getting boring—less fun.

In the real world, we live in a time where the "item database"—all the stuff we have—is bloated beyond all comprehension. Real-world policy-makers have focused steadily on growth, even after advanced societies achieved everything fundamental that growth could offer (safety, food, housing, health). It is now easy to see why: Growth is an extraordinarily cheap and easy (if deceptive) way to try to make an economy seem fair and fun. In times of growth, opportunities open up that were not there before. Moreover, lots of people have the feeling of "leveling up," of ending the game with more wealth than they started. Growth does not allevi-ate isolation, depression, frustration, or rage, but it does give lots of peo-ple the sensation of being richer.

The problem is, it is not at all clear that the sensation of getting richer and richer is perpetually fun. If anything, the pleasures of wealth acquisition seem to fade, unless the person goes mad with material lusts. Moreover, the structures and policies necessary to sustain the wealth machine impede the generation of fun elsewhere. Growth in the item database creates all kinds of game-play problems. It creates new oppor-tunities and gives people new stuff, sure. But does that lead to happi-ness? Let's say I'm a real estate agent and in my local market, about five sales opportunities open up for a typical agent every month. It's ex-pected that I go after each one. Now let's say there's economic growth. People are richer and they move more. As a result, ten opportunities open up per agent per month. My choices are to pursue five of those and keep my income the same, or go after all ten. If all the agents go after ten and I go after five, suddenly I am the poorest and least successful agent around. If the other agents go after five and I go after ten, suddenly I am the richest and most successful agent. Facing these incentives, every agent goes after the ten opportunities. As a result, if I want to even keep up in the real estate agent game, I have to respond to these new opportu-nities with new work. Otherwise I will lose my social status and reputa-tion. In dynamics like this, growth makes it harder for people to achieve a socially acceptable economic status; it forces us to do more work. Growth speeds up the pace of the running, but it is not clear that that makes the race any more fun.

In general, virtual-world designers avoid a general growth in mate-rial well-being. Rather, they prefer a structure that makes economic growth an individual experience within a non-growing economy. Everyone who starts as a penniless tailor gets the chance to make roughspun jerkins and robes, gradually working their way up to silk. There's always a market for those crude items you make when you're just starting out; the world does not become so rich that nobody wants anything less than silk. Each player gets the psychic reward of "making it," and indeed all players "make it" under roughly the same terms of reward and challenge.

Turning away from general economic growth would be a tremendously shocking change in macroeconomic policy. But a challenge will come. Do we really need to be wealthier? Yes, in the sense that individual people are happier when they overcome economic challenges and become wealthier as they age. But does *all of society* need to be wealthier? Does this individual story of success and advancement have to play out with more valuable toys when the son is playing than when the father played? The great wealth of society is in some ways a boon to humanity, but it has costs in terms of the environment and the allocation of human time. My argument is that it might have psychic costs as well, keeping us from having fun. The treadmill is turned up too high. The new scientists of virtual-world design, the fungineers, keep the treadmill at a casual pace, and they make sure its speed is stable across time. More and more people will find the virtual-world treadmill far more congenial to their lifelong happiness, and will demand that the real-world treadmill be turned down.

TAXATION

There are *no taxes* in virtual worlds. Just as charity and handouts are considered damaging to fun because they reduce the aversive element of coactivation—they remove challenge—taxes are considered problematic because they reduce the appetitive element; they reduce rewards. Almost every "sink" (a game mechanism by which cash flows out of a synthetic economy) in a virtual-world game is therefore described not as a tax but as a fee: a transportation fee, a storage fee, a broker's commission fee. Fees seem to be acceptable to players. They receive a service, and then pay a fee.

The real-world impact of this structure is not as strong as the ones listed before. It is already well-known in the real world that voters are far more inclined to agree to fees for services than for general-use taxation. Despite being well-known, this doesn't make such arrangements any easier to implement. Added pressure from tax-free virtual worlds will probably move the real world toward this kind of strategy, however.

In the real world, it is hard to imagine how a policy of no taxes could be made consistent with the policies of full employment and equal opportunity that seem so important. The government would have to find the money somewhere. Experience in virtual worlds suggests that the only place to find it would be through more or less invisible though broadly applied taxes, such as the sales tax. Obvious taxes like the income tax are less likely to sustain what little popularity they currently have. Moreover, if it is perceived that the economic game is becoming more balanced, the pure progressive impulse to income taxation may fall away.

INFLATION AND MONETARY POLICY

Inflation has been fairly common in virtual worlds. The technical reasons relate to the practice of full employment above. The way virtual-world governments make full employment available is by offering to create new money and give it to anyone who completes rote tasks. In effect, virtual-world players may always go down to the government building and shake the money tree there, walking off with whatever coins fall down into their hats.[4] No wonder there is inflation.

Despite being common, though, inflation seems to trouble no one. *Asheron's Call (AC)* had a vibrant economy that initially had a currency called *pyreals*. The designers' inability to get inflation in check meant that the effective currency for the world moved sequentially from the pyreal through a series of emergent currencies—scarabs, keys, shards—each lighter, more portable, and more laden with value than the last. Having the right currency became part of the game, as was the challenge of retaining the value of one's wealth stock. The inflation occurred most rapidly in *AC* because players could fairly easily cause more money to be created, whatever the money was, so that once something became money, the world was flooded with it. Woe to the entrepreneur who happened to keep his wealth as a stock of sturdy iron keys on the day that society adopted them as currency, for within a short period of time they would become worthless. Avoiding the penalties of monetary devaluation was one of the challenges of play.

Today's designers respond to this money flood by introducing various "sinks" in the economy to drain off what comes in by the too-numerous faucets. But if the "sink" is a horse that costs 1,000,000 gold pieces, all this does is incent the players to shake the money tree with all the more vigor. Faucet/sink monetary policy is in general not very effective at controlling the value of the coinage, especially when dupes are occasionally discovered by players. Dupes can flood an economy very rapidly, making the sinks ineffective. They also distorts prices, disrupting the game's economy. Designers dislike inflation enough that they do try to stop it.

In the end, most game currencies show a gradually declining value against the dollar over time. On the one hand, this indicates that inflation is persistent. On the other, it indicates that the currencies do maintain a fairly steady value. Inflation is not catastrophic.

What does all of this imply for contemporary monetary policy? There will probably be a mild crossover effect. Players are used to economies in which the currency gradually inflates, and so they will be less concerned with real-world inflation than they might have been had synthetic economies never been invented. The pattern of persistent moderate inflation already is comparable to that in the real world—there is always some inflation, but in wealthier nations it is rarely catastrophic, since the 1970s anyway. The indifference of players to inflation is consistent with the flirtation of western economies with inflation in the 30 years prior to 1980. In that period of Keynesian policy, governments hoped that loose reins on the money supply would spur job creation. What we learned from synthetic economies is that those Keynesian governments may have been able to pursue such policies because a moderate amount of inflation makes economic life a little more interesting, challenging, and fun. It is certainly no fun for people on fixed incomes, of course, but their incomes could be given built-in inflation adjustments. However, a widespread practice of built-in inflation-adjusting cements a given inflation rate in the economy, making inflation a one-way street: Once it goes up, you cannot bring it down again without a serious disruption to the real economy, causing income declines and job losses. And job losses are never any fun. Thus we might say that inflation can perhaps be fun in a real-world context, but because it is a lever that only moves in one direction, up, it is not an effective tool for fun management.

On the whole, a monetary policy targeted on fun would probably keep the same mix of austerity and relaxation that we now see. Austerity helps preserve both the value of the currency and the challenge level of the economic game. Relaxation may at times be necessary, though, for reasons of dynamic difficulty adjustment.

A NEW ECONOMY

Some of the policies I've reviewed here must seem like a leftist's dream, others the fantasy of the most radical right-winger. Yet these real-world applications of fun policy have an advantage that the fancies of political radicals never do: They have been successfully applied, by virtual-world designers, in genuine human societies. They are being tinkered with and perfected, even now, in an industry experiencing exponential growth and a vast expansion in available resources. True, the environment in which these new policies have been applied is itself a fantasy. Yet the people are real, and so is the social order they generate. Within that social order, millions of people are having fun. We could take some distinct lessons from all of this fun. In fact, we will probably not have a choice; these policies will either become unavoidable or second nature, as more and more people spend their formative years visiting virtual worlds. We should not be surprised when future generations of voters start to demand full employment, rapid wages, equal opportunity, and an end to general economic growth.

CHAPTER NINE

THE FUN SOCIETY

Fun policy speaks to issues beyond economic and social policy; it also makes recommendations about law, civics, and the policy process itself. Virtual-world designers consider the items topping the following list as central to the creation of a fun society; lower items are less central. You can expect to see these kinds of real-world changes as more and more people spend their formative years in virtual-world policy environments.

The policy issues to be discussed include:

- policy process
- scope of government
- myth
- law
- interration
- community
- access
- education

- segregation
- national defense, space, and diplomacy

POLICY PROCESS

Perhaps the most striking difference between fun policy and real-world policy is in the process of policymaking. Game designers deliberate briefly, then implement policies in test environments and tinker with them for a very long time. Real-world policymakers deliberate for a long time, then implement policies in the real world without any tests at all. Those who have experienced policy effects in both worlds cannot help being impressed by the difference in the policy quality that results.

Imagine a Department of Motor Vehicles office that actually worked. It is a breathtaking thought, I know. An impossibility. Yet those of us who have experienced the log-in and registration process for a well-designed virtual world have seen that similar bureaucratic tasks can be done easily. And while this is not the place to parse and analyze how license plates and title certificates should be administered, we know that the design of such real-world environments has not proceeded according to the norms of fun policy. Your local Department of Motor Vehicles office was thrown together by an overworked, underpaid government employee at some point back in the mists of time. Since then, legions of equally dispirited workers have filed through the environment he created, attempting modifications when they seemed sensible and possible, which was not very often. The result is a design hodgepodge, and for those of us who stand in lines, a completely and utterly disastrous social order.

Now imagine what a government office would be like if a game-design process had been used:

- The need for a new office is briefly discussed and agreed upon
- Complete resources for the design, testing, and construction are made available up front
- The design team is made financially accountable for constructing an effective design
- A preliminary design is constructed
- Several test environments are implemented
- Feedback systems between the testers and the designers are enabled
- The basic design is updated and tinkered with for a period of two to five *years*
- The office is opened
- Every six months, the office is modified to address any new concerns that have emerged.

Imagine if this design norm were applied to every government policy. Imagine this norm: "No policy goes into effect without at least three years of design testing." Or this one: "All public policies will be reviewed every six weeks, and modifications will be introduced to bring the effect of the policy better in line with the spirit of the enacting legislation." The mind boggles.

Contemporary government could also improve its communication with citizens by adopting practices of virtual-world builders. After the emergence of Lum the Mad, *Ultima Online*'s external critic, all game companies understood that it was important to host online discussion forums, so as to enable frank and open communication about player experiences and developer policies. While the companies' tendency to censor such discussions is deplorable, there's no doubt that the companies do get direct messages from the players. And it leads to the question: Why do we not have discussion boards about specific policy decisions by all organizations, beginning with government? If proposed Senate Resolution SR 563 makes me really, really mad, why doesn't the government provide an official site, fairly moderated, for discussion of the bill?

To advocate for such things is, of course, to join in a chorus that is hundreds of years old. Why do government agencies function so terribly? One reason pointed to by economists of a libertarian stripe is that the organization as a whole faces no competition. It is the government. It does not need to become efficient. People must follow its laws. But is this still true? We have new social orders in cyberspace. People who do not like the real world can spend all of their time in virtual worlds. Will this change how the government approaches policy? We can only hope.

SCOPE OF GOVERNMENT

From the perspective of fun policy, though, the main reason that government is so terribly ineffective is not the lack of competition, it is "feature creep," the practice of adding more and more unpolished features rather than polishing the features you already have. Real-world government employees I know are personally very dedicated to doing the best job they can. The problem is not their motivation (although over time they may lose some of their zeal); the problem is that the resources available do not come anywhere near what is necessary to achieve the goals assigned. One could have predicted exactly this outcome from within the perspective of the game design community. If you imagined a group of game designers who were told that they had, through the laws of taxation, an unlimited stream of resources and a design task with no deadline, you could easily predict what would happen: feature creep on an unprecedented scale. No task would ever be struck from the feature list. The group would attempt everything that seemed even minimally cool. This appears to be what the government does too: It takes on every task imaginable.

In design shops, feature creep rears its ugly head in sentences like "What we should do is . . ." and "Wouldn't it be cool if we could . . ." Young game developers are warned away from such thinking. They are told: Do not speculate on what might be accomplished. Stick with a very, very short list of goals, and then *deliver.* The objective is to consistently meet the goals you have promised, not to promise the moon and deliver some moon rocks.

Contrast this to contemporary real-world governance. No public desire goes unanswered by some policy proclamation or other. No aspect of daily life is considered unimprovable by government policy. In "town hall" meetings with voters, no candidate says "We don't have the resources to implement that. We might get to it in a future version, but not in this release." The answer to each and every complaint is that the government ought to do something.

We are told that this dynamic of super-government, the government that tries to do everything, is a necessary result of democracy. If people complain, they must be given relief. But that logic falls apart when we adopt a game design perspective on public policy. Complaint and unhappiness are not necessarily a sign that there are problems that *government* must *solve* for people. There may be a problem, yes, and perhaps the government should do something. But its actions are not merely limited to solving the problem. Maybe the right response is to change the problem so that people have an easier time with it. Or perhaps the people might even want to take on more of the problem solving themselves, or take on a different part of the problem. In general, a government informed by fun policy will not forget that challenges are good. The right response could be: "This system is working as intended. I know the challenge is making you unhappy right now. It is designed to do that. Keep trying. When you succeed, it is going to feel very, very good."

What fun policy recommends here is not a particular policy change, but a change in our attitudes toward public policy and the state. This is neither a leftist nor a rightist perspective, but an entirely new perspective on the scope of government. Leftists tend to think the state should always help. Rightists tend to think the state should never help. Future generations who are familiar with virtual worlds will lean to the left in thinking that the state should be involved in many of the challenges that people face. But they will lean to the right in thinking that once the proper challenge level has been set, people should be left to master it on their own. If life is a game, the government's job is not to help people win, but to make sure the rules are sensible and fair.

MYTH

The social order must have shared myth. In virtual worlds, there is an explanation for everything—why this city is located here, why members of this culture do not like members of that one, why this god favors hunters but not thieves. When people live together in a society, they are happiest if their existence, their togetherness, and the meaning of their actions are embedded in a bigger story, one that explains and justifies why all of these things have come to be and what they all signify. In virtual worlds, this purpose is served by the lore. The world has a backstory, a history, that the designers simply made up. Though completely fabricated, however, the lore serves its purpose. It allows actions to feel meaningful. This effect of the lore is not just a cool thing one finds in virtual worlds, though. Myth is the only source of meaning for human action, anywhere. Myth only works if it is shared in a community. The real world, too, needs myth. And some myths are better than others.

Fun policy would insist that a lore be agreed upon as an integral element of the design of real-world public policy, and it must be implemented universally within that design. The lore has to clarify exactly what is good and what is evil. It must create a map of meaning within which the actions of all the citizens make sense.[1] It should be stressed that the lore does not need to be imposed on the populace; indeed, it must not be imposed. It must simply exist in the backstory, be a part of the atmosphere. Citizens must have access to it when they wish to see it, of course. But it should just appear in bits and snatches, here and there.

A well-designed lore allows every player to find her place within it. *The lore excludes no one.* In most virtual worlds, for example, there is an explicit concept of race. Different races have different backstories. There are clear tensions among members of the different races. Nonetheless, *every member of every race is on the same side,* in the sense that there are some very bad things indeed out there that all players oppose. Even in PVP worlds, where players fight one another, it is still the case that there is a category called "monster" to which no players belong. Monsters are bad things. They must be relentlessly hunted down and killed. And all players are expected to take part in the killing of these monsters. The treasures obtained thereby are of value to all players as well. Thus even when players fight one another, their fighting is embedded in a larger map of significance, of us vs. them, of good vs. evil (though often not labeled as such), of bliss vs. chaos.

Such a map is considered absolutely integral and irreplaceable in the proper functioning of a social order. The one feature that the lore must have is consistency: It must be expressed in an internally coherent way across all player experiences. Players should never be placed in a situation where their actions necessarily contradict some aspect of the lore. If paladins are said to always protect the weak and innocent, a paladin must never be given a quest to torture a puppy.

What does this mean for the real world? It insists that we work hard to share values, and that our shared values should become an unabashed element of every fiber of the social fabric. This again places the game design perspective squarely at odds with both left and right. The right wants to put their god in the schools. The left wants no god in the schools. Game design says, come up with a god or gods that everyone agrees on (it *is* possible—it happens in virtual worlds all the time), and put him/her/it in the schools.

This is once again a deep, deep challenge to contemporary society. It insists that we do the hard work of coming up with shared values, norms, morals, and myths. That is an ugly prospect. Fundamentalist Christians know exactly what set of norms we should all adopt, of course. Modernist secularists are similarly insistent on the adoption of nothing. In this, game design sides rather against secularists. A fun social order needs a religion. At the same time, since the religion can exclude no one, it must permit citizens to stand in permanent opposition to the lore and yet still belong.

Is a crafted myth socially possible? Simulation theorists, such as Jean Baudrillard, certainly think so; their argument is that the real world is itself embedded in a crafted myth. Jung conceived a collective unconscious within which universal mythical entities exist in regular, interpretable relationships to one another. Joseph Campbell believed that all human folk myths played out a similar set of more or less universal tensions involving the journey of a hero. Tolkien argued that all myth *writers* (consciously or not) implemented a secondary version of a true, underlying mythical cosmos.[2] Putting all of this together, it seems theoretically possible to quite consciously create a mythical lore that becomes the background map of meaning for an entire culture of real humans. Tolkien's own mythical conceptions, indeed, seem very successful in this regard. They now form the basis for countless secondary worlds, occupying the attention and motivation of literally millions and millions of game players all over the Earth. Indeed, all of this might have been Tolkien's true objective: to provide modern humans with myths they could hang onto, yet whose content was consistent with the myths that modernity had discarded. Yet Tolkien was a writer, not a king. How would a government create a lore that became effective and "real" for the people it rules?

Perhaps the way out of this puzzle is to take refuge in the concept of play, in a collective agreement to adopt an as-if lore. Perhaps government might announce:

> We have adopted this shared lore as a useful pretense. We know not everyone agrees with it. We know it leads in bad directions at times. Yet we feel it is important to our sense of shared community that we have a shared lore. So we have adopted this one. We let it sit in the background. You'll notice it from time to time. If you have questions about some aspect of it, you can do some digging—there it is. And we are not ashamed of it; rather, it makes us proud. We energetically teach it to our children, to visitors, to new neighbors. The values conformity it implies is frustrating at times, but the comfort of having it exceeds those costs. It makes our lives feel more worth living. It gives us joy. It helps us have fun. And that is why we keep it.

This kind of acceptance would go some way toward embedding our day-to-day actions in a map of meaning. Such a thing is undoubtedly implicit in most contemporary developed countries; it is behind the phrase "That is what it means to be a(n) [insert group here]." Perhaps all that a game design perspective insists on is making this *implicit* shared myth into an *explicit* shared myth: something voiced rather than hidden. An openly practiced religion rather than a secretly shared set of assumptions.

Fun policy believes that shared myth is extraordinarily important, and shows how to implement it. Generations that grow up using virtual worlds will wonder why the gods of the real world are either hidden away or have become the source of conflict rather than community. "Bad lore" they will snort.

LAW

Game designers do not cotton to cheaters. In virtual worlds, *respect for the rules is a paramount social value.* It cuts two ways: Players should abide by the rules or expect extreme sanctions. But on the other hand, no rules should be imposed that cannot be enforced. Players often view themselves as engaged in a metagame with the designers of a world. The designers set up the rules, the players try to exploit them. Players constantly try to find game-breaking strategies that are nonetheless allowed by the code. If someone finds a vending machine that sells bullets for two coppers and another one that buys bullets for four coppers, energetic players will start pumping that little design mistake for money at such a rate that the entire economy will break down within a day. First they buy one bullet and sell it; four coppers. Use all four to buy bullets and do it again; eight coppers. Do it again; 16 coppers. Then 32, 64, 128, and so on. Twenty trips yields two million coppers. Fifty yields *two thousand trillion* coppers and the end of the economy. Oops! And it was all within the rules. Here, the code is key: It was a code failure that allowed players to legally earn so much money in such a short period of time. Lawrence Lessig argues that on the Internet, code is law.[3] Nowhere is this more obviously true than in virtual worlds. Designers attempt to enshrine every rule of the game in the actual code, so that it is impossible to break. If doubling your money that way was not possible in the code, it would be, in effect, against the law.

Rules that are merely written in the terms of service, to which players must agree, generally fall into two categories. One set of rules are proscriptions the designers hope players will follow more or less based on their own incentives. On servers designated for "role playing," designers hope that a role-playing community will evolve that will enforce in-character behavior through its own norms. The terms simply state that expectation in the hopes of inducing such a community to form. The other class of rules are ones that cannot be placed in code but about which the designers are dead serious. The term "dead" is explicitly used here: The designers will execute any character that violates such rules, banning the associated account. This punishment applies to such actions as verbal harassment of players on ethnic grounds.

I would estimate that the rules of the game in virtual worlds break down 80–10–10: 80 percent code, 10 percent terms provisions that are rarely enforced, and 10 percent terms provisions enforced through draconian measures. Thus, by and large, code is indeed law in these places. It is easy to see why: Code is an extraordinarily efficient way to execute law. One can declare something illegal and then simply prevent anyone from doing it. No need for arrest and punishment. The undesired behavior simply vanishes. Very cheap and effective.

The implications for the real world relate to the scope of government arguments above. We are learning that it is possible to construct social orders based largely on automated rule systems, in which the human element of enforcement is minimal. Where human enforcement is necessary, we see that the law is either not enforced at all, or enforced with severity. Such a system minimizes the cost of actually getting people to act within a certain set of rules.

The cost of law enforcement, and of governance in general, is high now, higher than it has ever been in human history. The reason is very simple: Average incomes are higher now. Economic growth has made humans wealthier and wealthier. As a result, the cost of human time has gone up and up. Governance in the real world is very labor intensive, and therefore it has become relatively more and more expensive as economic development proceeds. To sustain good government, we either have to pay for people to do it, or figure out ways for it to happen without human intervention, that is, to automate it. The first prospect is not working. The second is being explored in virtual worlds. The result of automated law in virtual worlds often feels like anarchy.[4] You don't ever see government—no police, no civil service workers, no mayors. Only the occasional "game-master" who has to come adjudicate problematic disputes. While governance is not apparent, governing is going on—in the code. People seem to like that.

The long-run influence of such a model of governance is hard to assess. To what extent could real-world law be automated? We already have cameras that capture traffic violations and send tickets. But eventually the traffic light could speak directly to my car and simply prevent it from moving forward when the light is red. This may or may not be good law, but it is definitely cheap law. Cheapness is a very powerful feature. Thus if the fun revolution makes any headway, Lessig's code law will have a future not just on the Internet, but everywhere.

INTERRATION

As the fun revolution spreads, one issue that will emerge quickly is the basic legal status of virtual worlds. What is the jurisdiction to which a virtual world belongs? Virtual worlds being on the Internet, we know the answer: Real-world governments are in charge. But it does not follow that the best thing for real-world governments to do is set policy in virtual worlds. In the real world, natural areas are set aside to protect them from economic development, and it might make sense to apply the same sort of policy to virtual worlds. Such a policy would be called *interration:* the legal creation of a new and special kind of territory. This is an analog to laws of *incorporation,* which allow the legal creation of a new and special kind of person, a corporation.

To see why interration matters, consider the contrast between two worlds that exist today, *Second Life (SL)* and *World of Warcraft (WoW)*. *SL* is conceived as a huge digital sandbox. Users are encouraged to make things in *SL* and sell them to other users for "Linden dollars." As we know, Linden dollars can be exchanged for U.S. dollars on a market that's been sanctioned and approved by *SL*'s owners. Those owners would be quite happy to see their users make mountains of real-world money by earning Linden dollars first and then cashing them out for real dollars. It is an integral part of their business model, not to mention the techno-libertarian philosophy that drives the project and motivates the entire design team.

By contrast, *WoW* is conceived as a fantasy game. Users are expected to explore the content of the world using a fantasy character they've created, making up a fantasy story of that character's life as they do. In order to make an interesting story for every user, *WoW*'s designers chose to allow users to get a sense of achievement and success as they explore the world. A core part of this success story is driven and enabled by a simple design decision: In *WoW*, every character starts out with *no money*, but as the character advances, she gets money with each new accomplishment. She can use that money to buy cool gear, animals, houses. All of those synthetic-material things make her feel like a success, much as real-world material possessions do. But they only have that effect if they are obtained fairly within the game's rule system. If the player's character got a huge house only because the character's owner paid some other person $100 real dollars for it, that house would no longer be a clear symbol of the character's success. And neither would anybody else's virtual house. In other words, if it becomes known and accepted that people are using real-world money to buy virtual houses, possession of a virtual house no longer indicates success within the game. This robs the designers' story of its punch, and damages the value of the game experience for everyone. Therefore, the game designers declare that buying in-world assets for real money is against the rules.

Suppose now a judge or a legislature faced the question of whether or not to levy sales tax on transactions in some other new world. Looking only at *SL,* the judge might see all games as an extension of the real-world economy. He might reason (correctly) that the fact that people are buying and selling virtual real estate for virtual dollars has no implication for the question of whether or not value is exchanging hands. It certainly is. If he has any questions about the value in terms of real dollars, he can look at the Linden dollar/real dollar market that *SL*'s owners run. From this perspective, he might rule that all virtual-world users should pay sales tax on the real-world value of what they exchange.

Looking only at *WoW*, though, that same judge might see the place as a fantasy game and reason that there's no place for real-world sales taxes in fantasy games. That would wreck the fantasy. Even though some people do trade their in-world assets for real money, the judge sees that designers ferociously combat that practice in defense of the purity of the gaming experience. From this perspective, he rules that no virtual-world users should ever pay tax on the real-world value of what they exchange.

Both rulings are wrong-headed, though. What the judge has failed to see is that some worlds are like *Second Life*, and others are like *World of Warcraft*. Same technology, different worlds. A nuanced treatment is called for. But in order to draw lines in the right places, judges and legislatures need policy advice—unless they happen to have been born after 1980, in which case the differences between *WoW* and *SL* would be obvious.

The advice that decisionmakers need is likely to percolate upward from various gamer communities who feel their interests threatened by certain legal cases or legislative proposals. Gamers and game experts will argue that virtual worlds are odd animals that need to be handled with care. Policies of interration—of special legal status for virtual worlds—will doubtless be part of these arguments.

COMMUNITY

For humans, isolation is bad, and modernity seems to provide isolation more than ever before. While no one can doubt that the freedom and independence most people in developed countries now enjoy is a good thing, the cost is awfully high in terms of separating individuals from any sense of shared community. An ideal community-individual relationship would be one in which we could always be independent if we wanted to be, but there would also be a community available at all times if we wanted to be part of a group.

Fun policy has solved this problem. The social and economic structure in virtual worlds is such that every person is her own master, yet working together is a norm. We tend to think that people sitting at their computers are isolated, but a reversal has taken place. Today, people sitting in front of computers are almost always interacting with other people. It's the people watching TV or stuck in traffic who are isolated, not the people playing in virtual worlds. In virtual worlds, ad hoc groups form constantly. It is considered completely normal and okay to walk up to a stranger with no introduction whatever and ask them to join with you in pursuit of a task. More permanent associations (guilds) become locations where reputations are stored and privileged communications can be conducted. These communication and reputation-storing tools are such that ad hoc groupings regularly and consistently succeed in getting all members what they want, even though each one is pursuing his own self-interest. As a result, in virtual worlds, you can be a steadfastly individualist person, yet also feel a member of a team, a guild, and a community. In our age of anomie, it is a truly remarkable achievement.

What it means for the real world is that people will start to show a preference for more team- and community-based social and organizational practices. People schooled by virtual worlds will expect the companies they work for to allow them to join in ad hoc groups with coworkers. They will expect a company culture in which teams form anew every day, indeed every hour. They will expect that team objectives will require their own class of person to be involved, and that there will always be teams looking for people with their skills. They will expect to be able to join and quit larger work organizations at will. And they will expect immediate rewards from their work in teams and groups, minute by minute.

Let's imagine for a moment what this would look like in concrete terms. Suppose we have a delivery company that is organized like a contemporary massively multiplayer game. Here's how it would work. First, the company would have a target size, and so long as the current employee base was below that target, anyone who wanted to join the company could do so if she met some minimum qualifications. The new worker would be invited to choose a class to occupy, such as Truck Driver, Sorter, Label-Reader, Pilot, Mechanic, Customer Service Representative, Accountant, etc. Each of these classes would be given a list of activities to complete and rewards for doing them. Drivers might get a list that says "Deliver a small package (five pounds or less) on time, one hundred points. Deliver a large package (more than five pounds) on time, two hundred points. For every ten successful on-time deliveries in a row, receive fifty extra points." Those points would accumulate frequently, too, providing the worker with the same kind of steady stream of positive reinforcement that games give. Scan a package, get a point. Answer a complaint email, get three points. Find a lost item, get one hundred points. Points would be used for buying resources within the company, and leftovers would be turned into wages. These reward schedules would be balanced in the sense that a normally talented person who put some energy into the position would net enough points to make a good living.

Now, in order for our driver to make money, she would have to have help from people who maintain the trucks and people who drive the forklifts that put packages onto the trucks. One way for her to connect to these folks might be to buy their time in a points market. The driver could pay the forklift operator five points for a small package and ten for a large one, or whatever the market would bear. She could also pay a maintenance crew two points per mile driven to take care of the truck. If things worked out as they do in games, however, workers would not use a labor market but would form teams on an ad hoc basis. Forklift operators and drivers know they need to work together. Let's say Bob the forklift guy just came up to the dock with a load of packages. He got some points for himself by getting them this far, but can get more by loading them on a truck. Jill the driver comes by looking for packages for her truck. They strike a deal: Bob loads his packages in Jill's truck, Jill delivers them, and they split all points proceeds both from the loading and the delivering. The team forms up, the boxes get loaded, and Jill takes off. When she gets back, they meet again and split up the points they made. If Jill was fast and fair, Bob will want to work with her again. Same for Jill. In the ecology of self-organizing teams, reputations for being a good worker matter a great deal.

New employees would have to work their way into the company just as new players work their way into games: they start at low levels and work their way up. The company would have training areas: local deliveries of very small items for very small payouts of points and wages. Chances are that such a trainee area would attract many workers trying their hands at various jobs. Most of those might decide eventually that there's nothing in the delivery business that they are especially good at or interested in, in the same way that many players decide that they are not very good at a certain game and move on. But some of these workers really take to it. They acquire reputations as good drivers, good mechanics, good forklift operators. Once they get enough points, they are allowed to look for bigger jobs at a different loading dock. If they do well there, they can move up again, working for major international deliveries and so on. If things seem too competitive at one level, a worker can just drop down to a different level, where pay per activity might be lower but there is more activity.

Management would organize all this activity by stating when and where it would give out points. If it is very concerned about lost items, it would impose big rewards for not losing items. If management felt that most work in the company ought to take place in teams, it would offer a points bonus for joining a team. If it is really concerned about on-time delivery, rewards would drop off rapidly when deadlines are missed.

In general, a company organized along these lines would operate in the weird emergent order that one sees in games. Instead of ad hoc bands of one hundred people marching more or less one after the other into a dungeon to do battle with a dragon and get treasure, it would be ad hoc bands of workers gathering more or less where and when needed to perform some work task to which explicit rewards had been attached. This is not how companies operate today, but increasing numbers of new workers will come to expect this sort of thing: working with whomever they want, whenever they want, at whatever tasks they want, and receiving regular rewards for every little thing they accomplish.

That's a big change for the workplace, but it will be a big change for civic culture too. As with work, people will expect to handle most public affairs as autonomous agents who are nonetheless expected and able to join in fluid ad hoc groups. Education would change in this direction; teachers would set tasks ("quests") and students would form ad hoc groups to complete them, learning along the way. The virtual world *Quest Atlantis,* developed by Sasha Barab at Indiana University, uses just this strategy to teach middle-schoolers from around the world about environmental policy. Kids from America band together with kids from Holland and Malaysia to address water quality issues in their virtual village. Almost without knowing it, they're learning about toxins. We are using the same method to teach the world's greatest writer. *Arden: The World of William Shakespeare* is a virtual world I am developing with a team of students, also at Indiana. Not only education will become more team-oriented and communal. Nightlife and sports will change as well, and even shopping. Imagine a post-revolution shopping mall. No more ambling alone past the glassy windows with vacant stares on our faces. Instead, the mall has been reconfigured as an adventure environment presenting us with puzzles that can be solved to get the best deals. The puzzles are such that they are much easier to solve in teams. Shoppers form into groups at the entrance and share information about our skills, resources, and objectives. Then off we go, bargain-hunting in packs. Of course, you don't have to join a group—that's up to you. You can go after the puzzles solo if you want. Or just shop, for goodness' sake. But the best deals regularly go to people who group up. This fact creates a mall culture in which sociality is the norm instead of the exception. The shopper is still free, but isolated no more.

ACCESS

In virtual worlds, the general concept is that all content is open to all players, but restricted by level. Everyone has the right to do everything, but that right becomes effective only when the player completes certain prior steps. Access to those steps is open to everyone, and indeed any person, almost regardless of skill or background, would be able to complete them eventually. Virtual worlds have legitimately created worlds of open access.

The best example is the leveling system: You can get to any content in the world if you achieve a sufficiently high level. To achieve higher levels, you must do things, such as kill monsters. If you kill big, tough monsters, or complete long and difficult quests, you accumulate many experience points and level up very quickly. But if you want to, you can kill millions and millions of small monsters—little bugbears, minor kobolds, and the like—earning a tiny number of points for each one. This is not challenging to do, and after several million kills, and several months, you achieve the top power level in the game. Thus even a person with very low skills but sufficient time can become powerful. Whether or not it happens swiftly or in a challenging way is up to the player. But the point is, anyone can do it.

For the real world, this kind of open access would reflect a significant change. It has already been enshrined more or less in contemporary society that anyone can apply for any job or any school or any contract. Most everyone has access to the competitions that matter. What is missing, though, is the assurance of eventual success. It is not the case that if you apply to Harvard 1,000 times, you will eventually get admitted. But that is just the difference between open potential access and open actual access, and the virtual world, like the real world, only offers the former, not the latter. I myself have never had a top-level character in one of these worlds. It takes too much time. Thus while I can potentially consume the content at the higher levels, in fact I never do.

But the inability of a time-starved fellow like me to succeed in virtual worlds is a sign that their approach to access is indeed important for the real world, in the following sense: Virtual worlds offer access in return for resources and skills that are different from those that grant access in the real world. To get into Harvard, you have to demonstrate brains or connections, but to advance in Norrath, you have to have so-ciability (to get into large raid groups) and time (to do the raiding). It is interesting to me that lots of people with brains and connections don't have time (and often don't have sociability, but I'll let that pass). Thus, access systems in virtual worlds test factors that are abundant among people who do not have the factors necessary for access in the real world. It is as if the virtual world is creating treasures for the sole pur-pose of allowing treasure hunts for those who do not do well in the treasure hunts of the real world. This is a tremendously laudable ser-vice. As is often said, "Life is graded on a curve." Only 10 percent of the pianists can be among the top 10 percent of pianists. Those who are in the bottom 10 percent will not be spending much time playing con-certs. This is bad; but virtual worlds now provide a system allowing people with time to become anything they want to be, including con-cert pianists.

How could virtual environments give everyone the experience of being at the top of a social hierarchy? The answer is straightforward: arti-ficial intelligence. AI imbues all of the characters in a synthetic world that are not being operated by real people. Often, these characters look and act very much like the characters of real people. We can expect that the roles performed by AI agents will get richer and more meaningful as computer programming and our theories of the mind improve. More-over, as bandwidth and computer power increase, game worlds will have more and more room to harbor AI characters. So one could imagine a virtual world that has, say, 1,000 real people in it and 100 million AI char-acters in it. In that sort of world, the 1,000 real people need not have too much difficulty being the star quarterback in the Super Bowl: one could just program the AI agents to be not so good at virtual football. The other

999 real people would be seeking some other kind of fame—Carnegie Hall, president of the United States, professor of video games. To achieve those heights, they would have to out-compete the hundreds and thousands of AI characters who have similar dreams. Alas, our flesh-and-blood heroes would just be better at the things required to get ahead; they would win these competitions, fierce though they might be. In the next world over, other real players are working on becoming emperors, or spies, or industrial moguls. While the poor AI characters lose again and again, all of the people are winners. We don't have that in real life. But it is possible in synthetic worlds.

Synthetic worlds thus offer an antidote to the real world's hierarchies; by multiplying the number of social environments in which hierarchies exist, and by populating the worlds with non-player AI competitors, they allow almost anyone to have access to top rewards somewhere. Fewer people in the real world will think of themselves as small, unimportant, frustrated, failed. Political, social, and cultural movements that appeal to these emotions will have less traction.

EDUCATION

The participatory ad-hoc grouping behavior I've highlighted above will have its effects on education as well. In a fun society, students in the real world will expect to be treated as autonomous agents. They will expect a more or less constant stream of tiny rewards—"learning points" (LP) as an analog to "experience points" (XP). LP will be better earned in groups, though, so students will team up to tackle assignments. The model of sage-on-a-stage will vanish, an effect of digital technology that has already been predicted within the education policy community. What is new here is the method by which the change will happen. Not through top-down policy reforms, but through a competitive pressure from virtual worlds. Students will spend most of their time in virtual environments and will have to be lured back to the real world to learn. To get them back, learning will have to apply some of the techniques of applied hedonics. Education will have to become more fun.

The content of a fun school will be similar to that of a fun civil society, as described above: education that's limited in scope, but polished by design, with open access, most rules in the code, ad hoc teamwork, and shared myths.

SEGREGATION

When they cannot find a ruleset that satisfies everyone, virtual-world designers resort to the practice of *dividing people by their interests* in order to maximize everyone's enjoyment. In the real world, this is known as "sorting," but also "segregation." It is not generally considered benign in the real world, nor in the virtual. Such dividing of the player base is to be avoided if possible. It is a last-ditch solution. On the other hand, it can be extremely effective. By creating two societies where there was once just one, both can provide more fun. For example, suppose one-quarter of the player base loves mimes and wants to see mimes on every street corner. The remaining three-quarters hates mimes and wants to kill them whenever possible. Designers would spend some time trying to come up with a mime solution, one that would allow mimes for the people who love them but keep them hidden from those who hate them. As a last ditch solution, designers might build two versions of their world, labeling one "MIME" and the other "NON-MIME." Players entering the game for the first time would then choose which world to live in according to their tastes.

The critical rule is that any such segregation must be based on play styles and interests, and be completely voluntary. The job of the designer is to create the two environments, and let the players choose themselves where they would like to be. The cost of belonging to one or the other must be the same. Otherwise, there is an access violation that would be intolerable.

This means that since real-world populations do sort themselves by location, the fun revolution will raise expectations that anyone should be able to live wherever they want. This collides with the reality of real estate markets, of course, in that not everyone can afford to live under the rule-set that they like the most. In this respect as in others, the game of the real world is never fair; rich people have more freedom to choose where they are living. In virtual worlds, the game is roughly fair, in that people can review the rulesets available and then simply choose which one to place themselves under. As more people become used to the virtual-world way of doing things, however, the expectation will grow that everyone have equal access to segregated communities in the real world. Income-based segregation will be seen as more and more problematic as time goes on.

NATIONAL DEFENSE, SPACE, AND DIPLOMACY

There is a certain class of public policies that I'd like to group as *adventurist:* Most voters tend to think of them as part of some kind of thrilling adventure or intrigue. Adventurist policies, more than any others, are likely to suffer a loss of public support as the fun revolution progresses.

Take war, for example. Will the nature of war change after the fun revolution? What will a "fun national defense" look like? It is possible that people socialized in virtual worlds will be more eager to fight wars, since that is what they do all the time in video games.[5] But precisely because they do all their fighting in virtual worlds, their desire to get into real-world fights will be minimal. Bluntly: Virtual worlds will satisfy the common bloodlust that has driven so many countries into so many stupid wars. There's also the likelihood that people having fun in virtual worlds will be hard to bother. If one real-world country attacks another real-world country, gamers are not likely to care. The problem for real-world policymakers will simply be to get everyone's attention. Most of the electorate will be too busy enjoying themselves in virtual fantasy lands to even respond to calls for real-world military operations.

Indeed, why not resolve our differences through the play of games? In Orson Scott Card's *Ender's Game,* space cadet Ender plays a game that turns out to resolve an intergalactic conflict. In that system, Ender's commands were routed to guns that shot real bullets. Why not get rid of the real bullets and resolve everything on a virtual battlefield? Fun for everyone; can be designed to yield a quick, decisive outcome; cheap; nobody gets hurt. If you lose, build up and try again. Form an alliance. The post-Westphalian order of European nation-states could have been sustained just as well through a three hundred-year-long game of Chinese checkers. The outcomes would have been the same, but millions of lives would have been saved. There would have been much more dancing, and drinking, and marriages, and babies. And the diplomats would have had a better time too.

The same sort of argument applies to space exploration. Many people support space exploration because they fantasize about a future that's been described in science fiction novels. We could argue about whether that future is plausible. My point is, very soon it will not matter any more. Almost everything that a person might want to do in space, they will be able to do, virtually. True, there will always be an exploratory and scientific element to space travel. But what about the romance of simply being an astronaut? Would it be very hard to make the virtual experience quite close to the real one? Probably not. What would it cost to build some kind of pod and put computer screens at the windows? Then run a virtual-world game on the screens. For all intents and purposes, sitting in a metal pod doing nothing for hours and hours *is* space travel, at least with current technology. A virtual-world implementation of space travel would not use current technology, though. It would leap ahead by centuries. The comparison would be between boring space travel in the real world, or exciting space travel in the virtual world. Facing that comparison, most voters will choose to support the virtual-world version rather than the "real" one. Real-world space policy will suffer, as will every other form of policy that receives support because it feeds the public's fantasies of adventure, conquest, glory, intrigue. Virtual worlds are better at that.

A NEW SOCIAL ORDER

We could speculate endlessly on the nature of a civic order founded on the principles of fungineering. As with the economic order, much of the implied change would be radical. None of it may be likely to happen just as written here. The ideas offered here point out a possible direction of change in the long-run. Taking the more immediate impacts into account is the job of the final chapter.

CHAPTER TEN

THE FUN REVOLUTION: ENDING THE POLITICS OF MISERY

The policy changes I have predicted will begin to hit home within a generation, but there's little awareness of them today. Current political debates make no mention of virtual worlds and show little or no understanding of what video games in general are about to do to society. It is fair to say that the policy issues relating to video games today can be summarized in one sentence: "Video games are harmful to children." This argument has become the premise for numerous pieces of legislation around the globe. The perceptual vapidity that lies behind such a sentence reveals how far we must go to get the world of policymakers up to speed with the emergence of the new technology. First we have to make them understand that video games raise far greater issues than they realize. Then we have to make them understand that virtual worlds raise even bigger issues. If only the core issue were whether or not kids should be playing these games— that we could handle. But instead we face a change in the social order. A fair assessment of contemporary politics suggests primarily that our society is really not prepared for what is happening.

That is consistent with the tone of these anti-game legal efforts. I suspect that such efforts are driven by fear of unknown technology, a powerful motivator that seems to be growing in leaps and bounds. This fear is about video games in general; fear of virtual worlds will be even more intense. If the technology of synthetic worlds takes root more rapidly than people become accustomed to it, it will stir up incredible emotions and cause heated debates. If so, contemporary debates about violence in video games will quickly be overshadowed by a much more thorough, and quite possibly bitter, dispute about the immersive worlds as a whole.

Among gamers, I sense a complete and utter dismissal of the concerns voiced by game-regulation advocates. In response to objections to violence, gamers roll their eyes. A similar reaction is given to the sentence "Games are addictive." Gamers generally have no respect whatsoever for such statements. They do not perceive them as fair and well-informed commentary. Rather, they consider anyone who says such a thing thoroughly out of touch—not because gamers are addicted themselves, but because the term "addiction" does not begin to capture the nature of the compulsion many feel toward games and virtual worlds. Consider a sentence like "A mother's love is addictive." You bet it is. No one can get enough of it. Anyone who isn't addicted to mother's love is a fool, or extremely damaged in some way. Not to be addicted to a mother's love is a bad, bad thing. I think these sentiments are similar to those felt by people who have experiences inside virtual worlds that are so rich, so deep, so meaningful that their experiences in the real world pale in comparison. A person who has had the experience of both worlds and found the virtual one so much better *ought* to return. In such a case, our complaints should be levied on the real world, for providing such a poor experience. People who love virtual worlds react to those who don't understand their attraction the way lovers of architecture react to the boors who consider the Cathedral of Rheims "some big old church." In a building like the Cathedral of Rheims, something indescribably sublime pervades the atmosphere. Something ethereal, transcendant, divine. Though intangible, it is real. Most people feel it. Some feel it very, very strongly. Others don't feel it at all. But it is there. A sentence like "Some people are addicted to these big old churches" reveals deep ignorance of a cathedral's impact on a visitor. Virtual worlds are not cathedrals, but they do transport people to another plane. They have a compelling positive effect on visitors, an effect dramatically misunderstood by many of those who have never spent time there.

This disconnect in the assessment of virtual worlds between gamers and everyone else is a concern because of the way the gaming population is growing, and also because the gaming population has universal and immediate access to an alternative social order where the politics pursued by "clueless" outsiders have no representative and no purchase. If real-world politics turn against the gamers, they will simply leave. Unless we try to stop them. But then regulating access to games would become the cyberspace equivalent of a Berlin Wall: a glaring wound in the social fabric that does nothing but heighten tension and lower well-being so long as it is allowed to fester. Rather than prevent the inmates from escaping, the gamers will argue, make conditions in the jail better.

LONGER-RUN IMPACTS

In the long run, the ascent of virtual worlds will have the effect of a mass migration, impacting both regions. Comparisons of lifestyles in different regions will be unavoidable. Even absent any serious policy debate, the contrasts in lifestyles will change expectations. People on both sides will ask: Why is it this way here and not there?

Leaders of the real world will have to decide whether to respond to these questions. We may simply insist on no change whatsoever. Or we may try to adopt some of what the synthetic worlds have done: Make the economic game fairer, open access to more people, provide meaningful activity for everyone, and so on. Different entities may make different choices. Some companies may rewrite themselves as large-scale virtual worlds, with leveling systems, earnings points, and ad-hoc group dynamics. Others may retain a top-down corporate structure. All we know is that virtual-world users are accustomed to choosing environments based on how much fun they offer. It will become increasingly difficult to run a classroom or a boardroom in a way that is not fun; no one will pay attention.

WHAT ABOUT FAMILIES?

Throughout this book, I have been consistently positive about games, to a fault. I take that stance because I believe a social order focused on fun offers us a better future than the social order under which we suffer now. There is one area, though, where virtual worlds make me worry: the family.

Games and virtual worlds make us happy; they paint the pleasure gloss on our sensations. But the pleasure gloss is not the same thing neurologically as mood. Mood is a longer-run state of mind. Depression, for example, is a mood disorder. You can make a depressed person happy, but this does not change the overall depressive mood she is in.

Our overall emotional temperament—joy, anxiety, depression, rage—depends critically on the nature of our emotional relationships with caregivers in childhood. Weak, disrupted, or pathological ties in the family system cause lifelong emotional and behavioral problems. The social order bears responsibility, too, because its norms and structures have a critical effect on the expectations and behaviors of all family members.

In other words, parenting is really important. Yet research by happiness psychologists has indicated that parenting is not fun. As a parent of two boys in diapers, I understand these findings. The joy in parenting comes in momentary bursts, randomly allocated within a long sequence of dreary admonitions, back-breaking pursuits, and the handling of human waste.

Here then is a very deep conundrum: Happiness requires that all people have loving caregivers in childhood. But when people are doing the caregiving, it is hard for them to be happy. If everyone comes to expect constant fun in their lives, who will give that up to be a good parent?

Things have evolved in virtual worlds that touch on these problems already. There are, for example, characters that seem to serve as replacements for parents. Most players will regularly encounter mentoring figures in these games: older men and women, nonplayer characters (NPCs), whose programming makes them tell players about important quests and send them off to complete them. As a cleric (a kind of priest) in *Dark Age of Camelot,* I would regularly be called back to a huge cathedral in the middle of Camelot City, where I would meet with Lady Fridwulf. She would give my character various quests to complete, and then reward him with increases in skills and new spells. It was something of a regular ritual: Return "home" to the cathedral and check in with the good Lady, who seemed to be closely monitoring my progress. Such an interaction is far from loving care, but for some players it is probably emotionally better than the care they have received from their real-world caregivers. At least it is reliable: The NPCs always do the same thing. And you can trust them: If they say they will give you 20 silver pieces for Gorgol's head, they will indeed give you 20 silver pieces for Gorgol's head. Whereas parents, being human, change their minds and break their promises.

Fun policy has another response, far more troubling. It gets rid of kids. Virtual worlds do not have children in them. In *World of Warcraft,* there are a couple of orphanages with waifs running around in them. The ladies who run the orphanage even give out little quests from time to time. But the little kids don't. They don't do anything if you talk to them, and you certainly can't play as a child. In most games you have this wide range of options of character types—humans, elves, lizards, cats, demons—and sometimes there's even an "age" slider bar that you can use to make your character old or young. However there no child types and the "young" side of these age scales doesn't go below 20 or so. However strong our motivation to raise children may be, no virtual world of any measurable success has implemented a system for creating and then taking care of progeny. I have heard the notion of virtual families discussed many times, of course. Designers are well aware of the possibility. But they say it "wouldn't work." That judgment should be read as "there is no way to implement a child-rearing system so that it allows all participants to have fun with it." I do not know of any attempt at family-building within a large-scale virtual world. New characters are not born or raised, they are created by pressing a few buttons. Voilà, a person.

Thus for all my pollyannish proclamations as to the good virtual worlds will do, I remain concerned about their focus on the immediate provision of fun. The most important job many of us have to do in life involves little moment-to-moment happiness but rather a more or less constant flow of work. That work eventually leads to positive hedonic states of satisfaction, contentment, peace. But in the immediate term, it is just work. Without that work, children will have a harder time achieving happiness. Thus a work ethic in parenting—a willingness to do a good job, regardless of whether or not it is immediately fun—is essential to the overall project of promoting happiness for everybody. Therefore there's a conflict between fun and satisfaction. Fun policy tells how to make people happy for a moment and how to make those happiness moments continue in an almost never-ending stream. It does not tell us how to make people achieve lifelong satisfaction. Nor does it tell us what we must do so that our children can be happy. The claims of fun must be set aside so that satisfaction and good parenting can go on. The pursuit of fun must be accompanied by the pursuit of deeper satisfaction, of a moral nature, produced primarily by things like the commitment of a parent to the well-being of his children.

But perhaps even here in this life-morals problem, we could say that fun policy provides an interesting set of guidelines. Suppose we say that our vocation is to start life as a player but end it as a designer, that is, a designer of the hedonic environment in which future generations, and most specifically our own children, will live. Designing games is not playing them—it is work, plain and simple:

> One of the most difficult tasks men can perform, however much others may despise it, is the invention of good games.
> —Carl Gustav Jung[1]

If we think that the job of crafting policy—for your family or society— is basically an act of game design, Jung's dictum calls us to consider it the hardest and most important thing we do for others. We are called not to solve the problems of others, but rather to create for them problem spaces within which they can realize their full potential as happy, healthy human beings. It is neither giving a poor man, or your own son, a fish, nor is it teaching him to fish. It is the act of creating a river environment in which the man, your son, would find so much joy in the act of fishing that he would teach it to himself. That is a tough assignment indeed.

If parenting and policymaking is game design, and game design is tough to do, then we have to wonder how we will motivate people to do the designing. If the fun revolution is to improve life in general, it must improve future lives, and that means that the broader lessons of hedonic design (which involve more than mere fun) must influence how we nurture. The focus on the immediate hedonics of fun must not distract us from the job of setting policies for our children and our society. Someone has to *build* the games.

Yet how do we convince people to stay in the real world and do design work? What keeps a father in his own home, if the fun-filled virtual world sits there a mouse-click away? All we can hope is that a new social order will arise that not only takes advantage of the policies of happiness from games and virtual worlds, but also encourages parents to parent well, and legislators to govern well, and not abandon the real world for the joys of dragon hunting.

BIG CHANGES

The social orders dreamed up and implemented by virtual-world designers are different from the social order of the real world. Why? The response that designing societies in a game is very different from designing societies in real life may or may not make sense, depending on how you interpret it. It makes no sense if the claim is that working within a synthetic environment filled with dungeons and dragons makes all the difference. It does not; it cannot. Surely it should be clear by now that the dungeons and the dragons are ephemera, icons, a mere skein over the workings of society. Replace the dungeons with office buildings and the dragons with bosses and you are back in the real world. Another interpretation is sensible, though. Perhaps it is the *perspective* afforded by the task of game design that allows a designer to be so socially creative. The virtual-world designer, as Richard Bartle tells us, has great ethical power when he designs his world:

> When all's said and done, the ethics of a virtual world reflect those of its designer. If *you* don't think about how to behave, about what's right and wrong, about responsibility, about rights, then why should your players? If *you* think ethics are other people's responsibility, so will your players. *Your* beliefs, *your* attitudes, *your* personality—they're all reflected in your virtual world. *You* have to take responsibility, because (at least initially) *you* are the world.[2]

Any of us who have worked in the area of public policy analysis can only dream of having this kind of power to translate our personal ethics into the ethical structure of an entire society. Yet this task is not even chosen by game designers, it is thrust upon them. Bartle is reminding his readers—inexperienced designers—that even if they try to ignore their role as creators of public ethics, a public ethics will emerge anyway, of which they, the designers, will be the only author. Game designers are necessarily responsible for the social orders they create.

With that great power, the tasks game designers have set for themselves have not been to create the City on the Hill, the New World Order, the Dominance of the Master Race, the Workers and Soldiers Commune, or any of the utopic nightmares that have haunted humanity's over-wrought imagination in the past two hundred years. They remained admirably humble and asked, merely, What kind of social order would allow people to have fun? By and large, game designers have eschewed any temptation to remake humanity and have focused steadfastly on the task of remaking humanity's sense of well-being.

In so doing, game design has spawned this new science of fun policy: a set of practical policy norms that, when applied to a society of real people, give every one of them a more or less lengthy stream of experiences that they would label as "fun."

We have guessed that the cause of this good time is a set of specific game structures: a play environment with challenges and rewards clearly labeled so that they appeal to survival drives, all of it embedded within a texture of meaning. Such structures appeal to the very nature of fun as I have defined it. If challenge is dynamically adjusted and altered for freshness from time to time, the fun becomes intense and long-lasting. If the fun persists uninterrupted for long enough, self-consciousness shuts down and the player enters a flow state.

Game designers have figured out how to make environments through which people easily find their way into fun-induced flow states; virtual-world designers have figured out how to make environments where flow emerges in an active social context. The core principles involve open access to experiences, along with constant employment opportunities, self-management with frequent ad hoc team-building, law in the code, and a level playing field.

These policy principles, if applied to the real world, offer a dramatic challenge to business as usual. They do not match up with contemporary policy. They do not match up with contemporary politics either. They appeal in parts to both the radical right and the radical left. A fun revolution would not only cause policy change, it would realign politics. But perhaps this is the time. The politics that structured the years in which I grew up—the cold war, the welfare state, flower power vs. the establishment—died in 1989. Those debates are gone. The new debate will be about the pursuit of happiness within the social order. What's the most important objective for society—to make everyone richer (the current objective in most nations) or to make them happier?

Our all-too-new experience with virtual worlds argues strongly for the latter. Why indeed are the policies of the virtual world so very different from business as usual in the real world? Even as we accept the answer—because virtual-world designers focus on human happiness while real-world policy designers focus on other things—that answer boggles the mind. Why in heaven's name has public policy ever focused on anything other than happiness? When did we decide that human well-being was not the most important thing?

Perhaps we have ignored happiness because we believe policy should pursue something more important. I have been careful throughout this book to avoid referring to proponents of fun policy as "hedonists." Hedonists by definition care only about pleasure, and we tend to associate them with pursuit of base pleasures at that. A hedonist is thought to be irresponsible and immoral. I would argue, though, that in a country where there is plenty to eat but suicide is a common cause of death, in a country where fewer and fewer children enter maturity possessing solid emotional relationships with caregivers, it is time to refocus on happiness. Money can't buy happiness or love. Keeping up with the Jones' is a shell game, a rip-off. The career ladder is a treadmill. The source of happiness lies elsewhere. On his deathbed, no man wishes he had spent more time at the office. In fact, dying people, I am told, speak exclusively of their relationships, of the regrets and fond memories left to them by their lifetime of being with others.[3] Our public policy should reflect that wisdom and help people live a life with fewer regrets about time wasted in pursuit of things that don't matter. A life of joyful sociality, playing games together if need be, would be much, much better. Virtual worlds are already allowing people to test-drive a world that's designed for fun rather than wealth.

Virtual worlds succeed in these comparisons because they are far more focused on hedonics than the real world is. That focus is a responsible and mature approach at this stage in history. Plenty of people attempt to be "hedonists"—pleasure-pursuers—without success. They usually learn that a life of dissolution, of casual sex and heavy eating, is hazardous for your health. "Hedonists" operating in that mode die quickly and in sorrow. Whoever told them that indulgence was the road to happiness was a liar. Those who focus on genuine human happiness, including those who design virtual worlds, advocate that lusts be tempered with love, that friendship become the cornerstone of activity, and that appetites be tempered with challenges. Happiness researcher Stefan Klein advocates a public policy based on "The Magic Triangle of Well-Being": civic sense, social equality, and control over our own lives.[4] Virtual-world societies today look as though they used Klein's triangle as a blueprint for construction: They encourage people to form communities, they make the opportunities for fun equal for all, and, being interactive, they guarantee a player's sense of control. No wonder virtual worlds make people happy. Their designers have apparently discovered through trial and error exactly what psychologists have discovered through research: that people are happy when their society is a community of fair play. On both practical and theoretical fronts, hedonics has become a serious field.

The happy lives that practical hedonics promises will also be *good* lives in every sense of the word, including being morally praiseworthy. Stanford psychologists Zeno Franco and Philip Zimbardo have studied ordinary people who do heroic things, and found that one key distinction between heroes and those who remain bystanders is that the heroes have actively imagined heroic actions in the past. This implies that if we foster a heroic imagination among people, we can expect more of them to do heroic things. Franco and Zimbardo say that video games are probably an excellent source of heroic imaginings, since they provide choice situations laden with ethically relevant consequences.[5] Those are the same things that allow video games to provide meaning, and in the context of virtual worlds, that meaning has the power of an entire society behind it. Not only that, but choice with consequence makes people feel good, and emotional well-being is probably the single most important resource for a person who is trying to make the right choices consistently. Happiness enables moral action. We have learned through virtual worlds, however, that causality runs the other way too: Morality is a key to feeling happy. A moral fabric, a "lore," has been found to be integral to the operation of a fun society. Perhaps here is where we find the incentive to parent well: in honor of our own desire to be loved and cared for as children, we will love and care for our own children, and the moral order will state clearly and with a loud, *shared* voice that that is the most noble action we will ever undertake. Perhaps parenting is the highest expression of a heroic imagination.

Through the revitalization of myth in the fun revolution, we will once again know that our choices have meaning. We will sense that our actions are relevant. That relevance can be applied to proper choices, such as the choice to love one another, to parent, to give. A map of good and evil causes our actions to matter, and that makes them fun.

RESURRECTING GOOD AND EVIL

In reintroducing good and evil to the social order, and doing so in a way that is acceptable to all, virtual worlds may be offering a deep and thoroughly laudable transformation of human life. Consider the story of a fictional person, Bob, whose interaction with virtual worlds is filled with meaning.

Bob: Mystic

Bob's real life is so boring it isn't worthy of being called a story. He's just Bob. Bob is 25 years old and he is a high-school graduate, an assistant manager in an office-supply store. But as soon as Bob gets home from work every day he throws the cheeseburger bag down on his desk and fires up his machine, loads a virtual world, and transforms himself into Abelaard the Paladin. This night, Abelaard will join an army of 47 other people, the realm's most powerful warriors, wizards, clerics, and rogues, in pursuit of Azengoth, the Demon of the Underworld, who has burst from his fetid lair to terrorize the game characters of hundreds of people much less powerful than Bob's Abelaard. As he flies his golden griffon through the blue skies to join with his army, Bob starts to feel so good. This. Is. Fun. Indeed this is the first moment of the day when Bob has actually felt alive. For Robert Montgomery Jones is at heart a noble young man yearning to make a difference, but his efforts to do so in the real world have been consistently and subtly shut down. He was too peaceful for sports and was taught to think of military and public service as fraud-

ulent activities. His religious upbringing stressed passivity and acceptance over the fight against evil. His teachers kept stressing that there
were no hard and fast truths, while simultaneously informing him
through mandatory standardized tests that he wasn't as smart as other
people. When it came to his career, Bob's mentors all scared the heck out
of him, filling him with an unconscious dread of income failure. A job
with benefits—that was the only acceptable real-world choice. But as
Abelaard the Paladin, this night, Bob is going to bring down Azengoth or
die trying, and thereby he will make a real, clear, and positive difference
in the lives of hundreds of people. For Bob, the virtual world contains a
map of meaning that he cannot find in the real world.

Bob's story, or actually his utter lack of story in the real world, points
to the depth of the transformation that virtual worlds will cause. In part,
this is a well-known story; Bob is exploring aspects of the self that the
real world represses.[6] But virtual worlds offer more than mere personality
exploration; they offer a mythical cosmos in which a personality can find
a reason to exist.

This aspect of virtual worlds may be their most powerful force for social transformation. In virtual worlds, we are consciously resurrecting the
notion of myth and directly embedding it in human societies. In thinking
about what this might mean for happiness, I return again and again to the
notion of a coming "Age of Wonder." Wonder, in the sense of miracle,
mysticism, and faith, may well be the single most important contribution
of virtual worlds to human experience. After the "death of God" in the
nineteenth century, the meaning of life for many became something of an
untended flower, socially speaking; individuals were left to find it on their
own. It is a difficult task. What, after all, is the point of Bob's existence? In
the real world, the answer is muddy, unspecific, and fraught with tension;

something to avoid in polite conversation, a fart at the dinner table of modernist sensibilities. In the virtual world, the answer is crystal clear: There are evil creatures, labeled as Evil with a capital E, and the point of Abelaard's existence is to be a weapon against them. His life is thereby noble. By extension, the life of Robert Montgomery Jones is noble too.

You may object and say that fighting evil in a childish game is morally empty. I disagree. First, merely stating that good and evil exist, and are not the same thing, is an advance over the current state of affairs in the real world. In the real world, most well-mannered people, people who wish to appear moderate and sensible, shy away from even speaking in such terms, leaving articulation of right and wrong in the hands of fundamentalists and sectarians. These days, far too many sensible and well-intentioned people have difficulty carrying on a sophisticated moral discussion. It's unfamiliar territory. Immersing Bob in an environment where right and wrong and good and evil are common terms at least gives him practice at thinking in such categories. But perhaps you feel that thinking in terms of good and evil is actually damaging to a person, that a more nuanced sense of the rightness of things is needed. Maybe; but the human mind does not seem very comfortable when it has nothing clear to care about. This is, of course, a Jungian insight. It is perhaps striking in this context to reread Jung's opinion of game design, along with an additional comment that he made:

> One of the most difficult tasks men can perform, however much others may despise it, is the invention of good games *and it cannot be done by men out of touch with their instinctive values* [emphasis added].[7]

The theme that fantasy provides meaning, meaning that is essential for human life, has appeared frequently. Bruno Bettelheim argues in *The*

Uses of Enchantment that fairy tales—precursors of virtual worlds—serve very deep psychological purposes, and that efforts to sanitize them or inject nuance into their categories can only rob them of their validity.[8] In fairy tales, the stepmother is evil, pure and simple. More recently, psychologist Jordan Peterson has argued that myth is a fundamental category of human consciousness.[9] The core myth is that there is a state of bliss and a state of chaos, the former to be pursued but never won, the latter to be feared, loathed, and fled from. Only through an encounter with both can the self-conscious organism motivate itself to do anything at all. By this argument, dread of evil and love of goodness accompany the human condition and cannot be removed from it. Yet the real world has become uncomfortable speaking in such black-and-white terms, fearful of the dire consequences that result from morally laden conflicts. But the problem there is not moral vision, it is the fact that we use guns and knives to fight one another. Thus perhaps if we move to an environment where fighting can happen but nobody gets killed, we may more freely speak of right and wrong. In virtual worlds, as in fairy tales, good and evil are labeled with bright, glowing letters. If nothing else, the labeling provides an environment in which those who feel the natural human need to encounter myth may do so safely.

The restoration of myth within virtual worlds goes deeper than mere labeling. Recall that Abelaard's quest involved killing a monster that was terrorizing others. In virtual worlds, those others are real people. They are running their little characters around, trying to do whatever it is they want to do, and here comes Azengoth, breathing fire on them and eating their cows. Stopping that kind of thing is clearly good. You don't need a myth to support this decision—everybody believes that if a bully is being mean to someone weaker, and someone stops the bully, that that is a good thing. The joy of the people at their deliverance gives the act meaning, even if you don't buy into the labeling of the monster as evil. Virtual worlds don't need the labeling to deliver meaning; they are ethical constructor kits where designers can create monsters that do things that everybody agrees are bad. The real world does not regularly produce settings in which someone, a monster, has clearly done something wrong, *and* another person is encouraged and enabled to do something about it. Virtual worlds produce such situations constantly—situations that engage the moral sense and encourage moral action, labeled as such or not.

Virtual worlds produce meaning in a third way, through sociality. The labeling of action creates meaning, the design of action creates meaning, and the embedding of action in a social context creates meaning. Maybe at first the rampages of Azengoth mean nothing to Robert Montgomery Jones, but as he spends time in this society, where people cry and rage when Azengoth burns their homes and eats their cows, he gradually comes to feel as they do. Sympathy for the pain of others is natural, and even if the pain stems from an abstract situation, we will still approach the people feeling the pain carefully, and with sympathy. Regardless of the source of pain, we treat pain with reverence, and naturally so. If you live long enough in a tribe where touching your hair is taboo, you will find yourself becoming quite uncomfortable with that act, and angry at your newly arrived friend for scratching his head all the time. The escape of Azengoth from his pens predicts a season of wailing in all the lands; dreading that wailing, Bob is motivated to become Abelaard, join with others, and do something about it. It is worth stressing that all of Bob's actions in the virtual world are *with other people*. The stereotype of the loner sitting at his computer still looks right—the guy is still sitting at this computer—but today he is not alone at all. He is in constant communication and collaboration with other people from around the globe. And all of those people spend a lot of time joining together to fight Bad Things, as a *group*. What a contrast this is to the real world, where isolated action has become the norm. Political scientist Robert Putnam has traced the gradual decline of social groupings as an element of daily life.[10] We still bowl, apparently, but not in leagues. The real world does not encourage people to band together. This must leave a yearning for a community of meaning, a yearning that can be satisfied in the community of myth-making found in most virtual worlds.

Still, in the end we might think of Abelaard's nobility as something pretty trivial. It's just a set of game-world myths, isn't it? How deep can they be? How much motivation, really and truly, can be wrought from a world where bashing orcs on the head is the main activity? Surely there cannot be any significant depth of moral meaning in dungeons and dragons. Or can there? These worlds owe much to Dungeons and Dragons and other role-playing games of the 1970s, which in turn owe much to the work of J. R. R. Tolkien. Few people know that Tolkien was a faithful Roman Catholic. He was also an apologist, a person who felt comfortable trying to get others to adopt his religious views. He was a long-time friend of C. S. Lewis, and was instrumental in converting him to Christianity in middle age. Lewis went on to build a dramatically public and successful career as an apologist himself, writing books, giving speeches, broadcasting radio addresses. He wrote the *Chronicles of Narnia,* a collection of unabashedly Christian fairy tales. In this he was emulating Tolkien, whose *Lord of the Rings,* nearing completion as Narnia was beginning, might be described as an abashedly Christian fairy tale. Earlier I suggested that Tolkien's purpose in writing his tales was to restore myth to the modern world. There is, in fact, substantial evidence to this effect in his life and writings.[11] As an orphan who witnessed the horrors of World War I firsthand, Tolkien loathed modernity for having carelessly tossed mythical meaning out the window. In a 1939 address to students and faculty at the University of Edinburg, he said that the creation of "Secondary Worlds," something he devoted his entire life to, was divinely inspired no matter who was doing it.[12] He would have called today's game designers "subcreators," and as such, agents of the king of heaven. Yet despite a clear sense of religious meaning, Tolkien did not take Lewis' approach of explicitly making his stories Christian. Rather, he set his tale in the mists of time and made it a simple conflict between evil and good. Middle Earth was not an effort to restore a specific lost myth, it was an effort to build a new myth that was consistent with the old myths that humanity had forgotten. As a new myth, separated but not divorced from its Christian roots, the lore of J. R. R. Tolkien has been dramatically successful. The vast majority of rights and wrongs one finds in contemporary virtual worlds have their roots in Tolkien. Elves are everywhere, and everywhere, they love trees. Orcs are equally omnipresent, and they perpetually love to crack skulls. Whatever we might think about this on an individual level, there's no question that Tolkien's constructed myth has succeeded in an incredibly wide variety of cultures. His synthetic map of meaning, expressed in games and virtual worlds, resonates around the world, from Japan to America to Russia. Something deeply Jungian is at work. People around the world love fantasy video games, and no matter who designs them, these games almost always involve hobbits, elves, orcs, and humans. What players and outsider observers don't realize is how very ancient these moral maps are, tracing their roots through Tolkien quite consciously all the way back to Abraham. Video games and virtual worlds are often subjected to scorn. Yet today, they are the most vibrant of vessels, carrying revered moral traditions into the future. The myths one finds in virtual worlds deserve not scorn but reverence. Through single-player games, players encounter our most hallowed traditions; through virtual worlds, they can once again live them.

Virtual worlds are on the path to becoming the most powerful source of personal meaning in the contemporary world. The changes that result might well be compared to the ones unleashed by Luther's 95 Theses: not just a fun *revolution*, but a fun *reformation*.

BEYOND FRUSTRATION, BOREDOM, AND EMPTINESS

I've argued that fun will become a core objective of our society, that we will eventually integrate the lessons of social-level game design in the way we organize education, business, and government. Change will be traumatic. It might well be resisted. I doubt, however, that any resistance will make a difference. We are not really going to have any choice in the matter. The exodus into virtual worlds may seem like a distraction today, but it will grow from a distraction into an amusement, from there into a challenge, and from there into a revolution.

While I am concerned about the trauma of change, I think the direction in which virtual worlds are pointing society is a good one. For too long, our society has been paying attention to things that don't matter—such as wealth—and ignoring things that do matter—such as emotional well-being. The evidence has grown over the last 50 years that the focus on things like money has put us off track. Hedonic psychologists and economists have had trouble connecting happiness to incomes and shiny cars. Researchers in social policy have found that money has a very small effect on a kid's lifetime prospects; in comparison, the family's relationships have a massive effect.[13] John Kenneth Galbraith wondered in 1958 why we didn't use all of our riches to eliminate poverty, but our social programs of the 1960s showed that distributing money doesn't make poverty go away. We've generally assumed that because people avidly pursue money (and associated ephemera, like fame and power), a social order focused on getting money would make everyone happy. It didn't. It's been making everyone unhappy, as a matter of fact. The game is too frustrating for some people, too boring for others, and completely empty and devoid of meaning for most. We didn't see that society was a game design problem all along, that the solution was not to constantly put more money into the game but to improve the way the game plays. Instead, we have ignored the game design problems that confront us, focusing instead on the scores of this old, outmoded, money-hunting game.

The coming exodus into virtual worlds will force us to change. The society that emerges in the real world will have to become more fun than the society we have now. Because games and virtual worlds have learned how to help people learn and work and socialize while having fun, the new society will also probably be better educated, more productive, and more civically engaged. I hope we will parent as well or better. Our task is to prepare for the revolution by further developing the new science of fun policy, seeing what we can accomplish with the tools that virtual-world designers have created. Doing so, we will improve our understanding of the world to come. More important, though, we may well discover some new, exciting, and beneficial things about how our society works, and how it can make every one of us happier.

EPILOGUE

An elected member of the U.S. government—I'll call him Senator Doe—heard about virtual worlds and had one of his assistants contact me for background information. The senator had a track record in family issues and had already issued the following press release in 2005, which I reprint verbatim from the senator's website:

* * *

FOR IMMEDIATE RELEASE

SENATOR DOE, VIDEO GAME EXPERT, SUPPORTS RE-STRICTIONS ON SALES OF BAD VIDEO GAMES TO MI-NORS AND ANYONE WHO KNOWS MINORS

In response to the national epidemic in high school shoot-ings, Senator John Doe today called for broader control over all the video games that portray nothing but random killing and acts of senseless violence. "It may surprise some people, but I have played some of these games myself," the senator said in a statement. "I have been in *Sim City*, and *Civilization*, and I have seen my children and nephews playing. So I know quite a lot about these games. And from what I have seen, the games the kids are playing are violent and not good for anybody."

The senator pointed to games like *Grand Theft Auto:* "The whole point of these kids' games is to get your prostitute into your car, take your drugs, and then kill her. That's just not something kids should be exposed to." Senator Doe offered on his website a series of videos, 15 seconds each, from three completely different games: *Grand Theft Auto, Doom 3,* and *Grand Theft Auto: San Andreas,* showing how senseless, meaningless violence against innocent people has come to permeate all games. "Clearly, kids who play these games will go on to kill real people, perhaps beginning only with their prostitutes but then moving on to our neighbors, friends, and loved ones. Only by preventing kids from playing video games will we be able to keep our society safe and at peace."

The senator supports Senate Bill 1337, which would impose fines on retailers who sell certain restricted video games to minors or anyone with access or likely close physical proximity (within five feet) to a minor. Restricted games would include only those in which direct or indirect force is exerted by the player against moving objects in the virtual environment. "We're not being draconian with this bill," the senator said. "We just want to limit kids' access to this content, which anyone can see will ruin them for life."

* * *

Senator Doe's assistant, whom I'll call Clarice, wanted advice and guidance in understanding the virtual-world phenomenon. She told me that the senator was proud to have already made an appearance in *Second Life,* a nonfantasy, nongame virtual world. I was somewhat nonplussed, since, by the time she had called in early 2007, the number of CEOs, journalists, pundits, judges, and politicians who had made the standard 27-second appearance in *Second Life* had already topped 150,000. What Clarice had heard, and wanted to know about, was the possibility that there might be some other venue of virtual-world interaction besides *Second Life*. I told her that the obvious candidate would be the seven million–person *World of Warcraft* (or *WoW*). Indeed, by early 2007 it had become hard to find any virtual world other than *Second Life* or *WoW*. Word on the street was that those who tried to open accounts in other worlds were being swept off to reeducation camps until they learned the error of their ways. Loathe to submit a hapless senatorial assistant to such a fate, I dutifully offered to take her on a tour of *WoW*. "The senator wants to see the gratuitous violence there, and make a brief statement," she explained. I explained to her how to create accounts and characters, and we arranged for a time to log in together and a place to meet in the virtual world.

What follows is my transcript of our chat during the session. Readers should understand that the text in virtual-world chat comes in different colors depending on the source. Person-to-person private messages might be white, while messages that can be heard by everybody in the vicinity might be red. Messages seen by everyone in a player group might be purple. The person sending the message chooses what channel to send it in—private, public, or group. In addition, the game server sends information messages, such as "It begins to rain," in their own color. Since this is a black-and-white book, I have used typefaces to represent the message source. In what follows, I have joined a play group with Senator Doe and his assistant Clarice; our group chat is in regular typeface. Statements in the "say" channel, which are "out loud" and can be seen by everyone nearby, are in **bold**. Person-to-person private statements are in *italic*. Finally, statements in ALL CAPS are server messages.

*   *   *

BEGIN CHAT LOG TRANSCRIPT

Comolan: hi this is ted, how are you two

Sendoe: Hello. I am fine. How are you?

Comolan: great want to get started?

Clarisseee: The Senator will have about 30 minutes today.

Comolan: kk

Clarisseee: He will begin with a brief statement.

Sendoe: Please take us to the place where the CEOs and other Members of Congress have made their speeches here.

Comolan: . . .

Comolan: wow doesn't really have that, sir

Clarisseee: Well, I think the Senator is just looking for the virtual world equivalent of the press room.

Comolan: k how about lion's pride inn, a tavern in goldshire. there's people there.

Clarisseee: I don't think a tavern would set the right image.

Sendoe: I had the impression that this had all been worked out.

Clarisseee: Very sorry sir.

Comolan: no sweat, there's a public square in stormwind where ppl hang out

Sendoe: Wait, what's a "ppl"?

Comolan: sorry, gamer jargon. abbreviation for "people." when you play these games and have to type your whole conversation you shorten stuff

Sendoe: Yes. I see. It is alright if I shorten my sentences then. I will try to avoid verbosity in subsequent transmissions!

Comolan: ya good

Clarisseee: How do we get to Stormreach then?

Comolan: follow. use w a s d keys to steer.

Sendoe: Very good. I would like to make my statement to a substantial audience if possible, so now I will follow you to this "virtual city" of which you speak.

Sendoe: Where are you?

Comolan: on road, half-way there. follow

Sendoe: Can't see you.

Clarisseee: Senator, go forward. Towards my guy.

Sendoe: wwwwwwwwwwwwwwwwwwwwwwwwwwwwwwwwwwwwwwww

Sendoe: Ah yes.

Comolan: use minimap to orient

Sendoe: What building to I go into to find this map

You say to Clarisseee: thought you said he knew what to do

Clarisseee says to you: We were able to scan the audience from the stage and type his speech in Second Life. I did not know we would have to move like this.

Sendoe: where map

Comolan: upper right hand corner of screen. center dot is you, other dots are me and clarice

Sendoe: Ah. Yes I see it now.

Maia: Awesome, thanks for sharing.

Sendoe: Who are you?

Comolan: senator, you're in the say channel. type /p to return to party default

Maia: A pretty little nothing, who are you sweetie?

Sendoe: What's "party default"?

Maia: my modus operandi, that's what it is

You say to Clarisseee: lemme go get him. follow

Comolan: senator, can u see me now? behind the elf

Sendoe: Yes, I can see you. My goodness, she is very pretty.

Maia: How sweet! "And he is both handsome and charming!"

Comolan: again, sen, you need to get out of the say channel.

Comolan: follow pls

You say to Clarisseee: cant get him away from this elf

Clarisseee says to you: Who is the elf?

Sendoe: Alright, I will follow you.

Sendoe: But she is wearing next to nothing.

Maia: You got that right, honey.

Maia: whaddya think of this?

MAIA DANCES WITH SENDOE

You say to Clarisseee: how should I know

Clarisseee: Senator, let's follow Comolan to the city.

Senator: In a moment. What does "cyb0r" mean?

Comolan: senator, please type /p now

Sendoe: get this woman away from me

Clarisseee: where are you going sir

Sendoe: ddddddddddddddddddddddddddddddddd

You say to Maia: cmon leave him alone

Maia says to you: n00bs lol

Comolan: ur in the woods, get back to the road sir

Clarisseee: what in woods

Sendoe: Where are you?

Maia: Over here, sweety!

Comolan: there are mobs in the woods

Clarisseee: Mobs?

Sendoe: Mobs would work. Is there a platform to speak from as well?

Comolan: no, these are monsters

Argfark: wassup yall

STARVING WOLF SLASHES SENDOE FOR 6 POINTS OF DAM-
    AGE

Comolan: run

Comolan: senator, run away from it

STARVING WOLF ATTACKS SENDOE. SENDOE DODGES.

Sendoe: ssssssssssssssssssssssssssssssssssss I am trying to evade it

Argfark: yowza n00b spam warning wassup yall

Comolan: run you guys don't stand there

STARVING WOLF CRITS SENDOE FOR 16 POINTS OF DAMAGE.

SENDOES DIES.

You say to Clarisseee: great

Argfark: 18 ranger lfg

Sendoe: Where am I?

Argfark: goldshire, n00blet

Comolan: you've been brought back to life in a cemetery. we will come get you. stay put. clarisseee, follow

Clarisseee: He is getting angry.

Clarisseee: You'll need to get us to some sort of political or corporate space immediately.

Comolan: as i said, this world is not designed for political and corporate appearances.

Sendoe: I see an angel. Where are you?

Comolan: right behind you. click on the angel to come back to life.

Billybong: [sings] are you my angeeelllll . . .

Purdy: rofl

Sendoe: What is rofl, or who is rofl?

Maia: You are, sweetie nub

Comolan: it means 'rolling on the floor laughing. senator please stop sending messages into the public channel. just type /p and then anything

Sendoe: test

Comolan: that's it

Comolan: ok please follow

Comolan: this way pls

Sendoe: wwwwwwwwwwwwwwwwwwwwww

TIMBER WOLF CRITS SENDOE FOR 16 POINTS OF DAMAGE.
SENDOE DIES.

Sendoe: god damn

Comolan: you need to just follow me

Clarisseee: We were following you. You led us into the wolves.

Sendoe: where is that god damn wolf

Comolan: n o I led you onto the road. you need to move forward
and turn

Sendoe: where is that god damn wolf

Comolan: ?

Comolan: well, theyre all over here, really

Sendoe: there's that god damn

Comolan: wait you need to equip your mace

SENDOE PUNCHES TIMBER WOLF FOR 1 POINT OF DAMAGE.

TIMBER WOLF ATTACKS SENDOE. SENDOE DODGES.

Comolan: wait let me tell you how combat works

CLARISSEEE PUNCHES TIMBER WOLF FOR 1 POINT OF DAM-
AGE.

Comolan: wait

SENDOE PUNCHES TIMBER WOLF FOR 1 POINT OF DAMAGE.

TIMBER WOLF SLASHES SENDOE FOR 6 POINTS OF DAMAGE.

CLARISSEEE PUNCHES TIMBER WOLF FOR 1 POINT OF DAM-
AGE.

Comolan: guys equip swords or you will die

SENDOE PUNCHES TIMBER WOLF FOR 1 POINT OF DAMAGE.

TIMBER WOLF SLASHES SENDOE FOR 6 POINTS OF DAMAGE.

Sendoe: god damn have mace not sword

CLARISSEEE PUNCHES TIMBER WOLF FOR 1 POINT OF DAM-
AGE.

COMOLAN ATTACKS TIMBER WOLF. TIMBER WOLF DODGES.

SENDOE PUNCHES TIMBER WOLF FOR 1 POINT OF DAMAGE.

TIMBER WOLF SLASHES SENDOE FOR 8 POINTS OF DAMAGE.

Comolan: you're a healer anyway, ur not supposed to be attacking

CLARISSEEE PUNCHES TIMBER WOLF FOR 1 POINT OF DAM-
AGE.

SENDOE DIES.

COMOLAN SLASHES TIMBER WOLF FOR 12 POINTS OF DAM-
AGE.

TIMBER WOLF DIES.

Sendoe: god dammit

Clarisseee: Senator, remember, count ten.

Sendoe: god damn sonuva

Comolan: very sorry sir. didn't get a chance to explain it, but, as a
healer you are supposed to stay in the back. let us fight. you cast
healing spells only. not supposed to fight. your role is peaceful

Clarisseee: The senator was not supposed to be exposed to violence.

Sendoe: you can take your peaceful and shove it up your ass

SENDOE LOGS OUT

Clarisseee: This is worse than Grand Theft Auto. He stole several cars
there and was pretty happy.

Comolan: ya. well, this place has other people in it

Clarisseee: But equally violent, obviously. I think we have seen
enough.

Comolan: but wait, there's thousands of hours of exploring you have
to do. millions of people. player markets, player politics.

Clarisseee. No. It's like a book. What's on the first page is all you need
to see.

Comolan: . . .

Clarisseee. We won't need to go through this again. But you obviously need some help, if you can't handle this place.

Comolan: okies. take care.

CLARISSEEE LOGS OUT.

*   *   *

Soon after this virtual-world interaction, the senator's office issued another press release.

*   *   *

FOR IMMEDIATE RELEASE

SENATOR DOE, VIRTUAL-WORLDS EXPERT, CALLS FOR
RESTRICTIONS ON ACCESS OF DECENT PEOPLE TO BAD
VIRTUAL WORLDS

In a speech today to a water fountain outside his office in
Washington, video games expert Senator Doe reported on his recent researches into the violent world of virtual-world games.
"These places are dens of iniquity. Innocent people are accosted
by loose women and attacked by wolves and killed. Any normal
person exposed to this environment quickly turns into a raving
maniac and succumbs to the temptations of violence himself.
The entire technology should be banned."

The senator made exception for good virtual worlds like
Second Life. "In *Second Life,* there was a stage to stand on and
several people there with their characters, who listened politely
to my speech. There was not a single Timber Wolf there who attacked me for no reason." In light of his expertise, the senator
recommended that legislators listen only to him and draw their
lessons entirely from his ten-minute experience in the virtual
world *World of Warcraft.* "Subtle distinctions will have to be
made. Worlds that have heroic fantasy in them, such as *World of
Warcraft,* are probably the greatest source of danger. But there is
no reason to restrict access to worlds without Timber Wolves in
them."

Senator Doe announced that he is crafting a bill that would
make these subtle distinctions concrete in legislative language.
"We will identify good worlds by whether or not they have timber wolves in them. Worlds without wolves are good. Whereas,
worlds with violent animals of all kinds will fall strictly on the
bad side. The Federal Trade Commission will decide whether a

world might offer dangerous opportunities for violence, primarily by looking for wolves."

Senator Doe's bill is considered a central plank in a new political movement to combat fantasy in all its forms. "Experts report that fantasy leads to imagination, and we all know that imagination leads to planning and planning to execution in the real world." The senator's crusade aims to protect America from the horrors of a reality warped by fantasy. "Unless we put a stop to this now, people may use their imaginations to play out all kinds of violent heroic fantasies, like fighting a timber wolf. Some people might get obsessed with being a hero in that sort of environment. They might find that the violence endows their actions with meaning, and then give up on our reality entirely. And our reality of shopping malls, traffic jams, cubicles, and cookie-cutter housing would be a terrible thing to lose."

* * *

Author's note: The preceding was a jest, a story about an encounter between professional, serious people and the strange world of massively multiplayer games. If the chat text seems incomprehensible, it only means that there's a new language developing and you don't know it (yet). I suspect, though, that the press releases are comprehensible and, indeed, have the tone of verity about them. To make the point, I'll close with another press release, this time a real one, from real politicians. It's about children and violence in ordinary video games.

December 16, 2005
SENATORS CLINTON, LIEBERMAN AND BAYH INTRODUCE FEDERAL LEGISLATION TO PROTECT CHILDREN FROM INAPPROPRIATE VIDEO GAMES

Washington, DC—With just over a week left in the holiday gift shopping season, Senators Hillary Rodham Clinton, Joe Lieberman and Evan Bayh, joined by parents, advocates and experts, introduced legislation designed to prohibit the sale of inappropriate video games to children. In unveiling the bill, the Senators underscored that video game content is getting increasingly violent and sexually explicit, yet young people are able to purchase these games with relative ease and parents are struggling to keep up with being informed about the content. The Senators emphasized that their legislation will put teeth in the enforcement of video game ratings, helping parents protect their children from inappropriate content. They were joined in making the announcement by April DeLaney, Director of the Washington Office for Common Sense Media; Norman Rosenberg, President and CEO of Parents Action for Children; and Dr. Michael Rich, Director of the Center on Media and Child Health at Children's Hospital in Boston and Assistant Professor of Pediatrics at Harvard Medical School, in a show of support for the legislation.

"The holiday season is a particularly important time to raise awareness of this issue. Video games are hot holiday items, and there are certainly wonderful games that help our children learn and increase hand and eye coordination. However, there are also games that are just not appropriate for our nation's youth," said Senator Clinton. "This bill will help empower parents by making sure their kids can't walk into a store and buy a video game that has graphic, violent and pornographic content."

"The content of many cutting edge games is becoming more and more vivid, violent, and offensive to our most basic values," Lieberman said. "We are not interested in censoring videos meant for adult entertainment but we do want to ensure that these videos are not purchased by minors. Our bill will help accomplish this by imposing fines on those retailers that sell M-rated games to minors, putting purchasing power back in the hands of watchful parents."

"Many parents are being stretched thin trying to provide a good life for their children while protecting them from a coarsening culture," Senator Bayh said. "Our legislation will give parents a hand by requiring retailers to abide by the ratings that are meant to keep children from purchasing violent video games."

The Clinton-Lieberman-Bayh bill, the Family Entertainment Protection Act, prohibits any business from selling or renting a Mature, Adults-Only, or Ratings Pending game to a person who is younger than seventeen. On-site store managers would be subject to a fine of $1,000 or 100 hours of community service for the first offense; $5,000 or 500 hours of community service for each subsequent offense. The bill also requires an annual, independent analysis of game ratings and requires the Federal Trade Commission (FTC) to conduct an investigation to determine whether hidden content like in *Grand Theft Auto: San Andreas* is a pervasive problem and take appropriate action. In addition, the bill will help ensure that consumers have a mechanism to file complaints with the FTC and that the FTC will report these complaints to Congress. Finally, the bill authorizes the FTC to conduct an annual, random audit of retailers to monitor enforcement and report the findings to Congress.

Senator Clinton was motivated to take action on this issue when it was revealed in July that Rockstar Games had embedded illicit sexual content in the video game *Grand Theft Auto: San Andreas*. This game had received a Mature rating from the Entertainment Software Ratings Board (ESRB), which was unaware of the embedded content. When the content was revealed, Senator Clinton called on the FTC to investigate the source of the content and announced that she would work to develop legislation to address this problem. Senator Lieberman wrote to Rockstar games asking them to come clean on whether the material was embedded in the game. Rockstar Games subsequently recalled the game.

Representative Joe Baca (CA), who has introduced legislation in the House to improve the video game ratings system, praised Senator Clinton for her involvement in this issue. "I applaud Senator Clinton for introducing this legislation, and I look forward to working with her to help parents protect their children from exposure to inappropriate and harmful images."

Illinois, Michigan, and California have all passed state laws to prohibit the sale of violent video games to minors.[1]

* * *

In light of the poor grasp these legislators seem to have on the phenomenon of simple video games, it is sobering to consider how their lack of comprehension will manifest itself when the still more complex phenomenon of synthetic worlds appears on the political radar.

NOTES

PREFACE
1. I would also point readers to John Beck and Mitchell Wade, *Got Game: How the Gamer Generation Is Reshaping Business Forever* (Harvard Business School Press, 2004), for two business school professors' thoughts on the impact of games on business. I am not the only one who believes games are going to change the real world.

CHAPTER ONE
1. While most scholars and pundits in this area use "virtual world," "synthetic world" more clearly captures what these places are: worlds inside computers, completely designed and constructed by human beings. Are they "virtual"? It's hard to say, because the word "virtual" has such an ambiguous meaning. Are they "synthetic," that is, crafted, constructed, artificial? Absolutely. Nonetheless, I will use the terms interchangeably. Also, as yet there's no generally accepted term for people who spend a lot of time in these places; we might call them *synthrims* for "synthetic pilgrims." Other suggestions have been "players" (since most are playing a game), "deckers" (from the holodeck), "gaters" (from the concept of dimensional gates), or "vitizens."
2. This is not the place for an exhaustive introduction to synthetic worlds and how they operate. For that, readers should refer to my first book, *Synthetic Worlds*. Even better: Readers who want to understand this phenomenon should just play. Practical virtual reality has to be experienced in order to be appreciated.
3. Edward Castronova, "On Virtual Economies," *Game Studies* 3(2) (2003), http://www.gamestudies.org/0302/castronova/.
4. Sherry Turkle, *Life on the Screen: Identity in the Age of the Internet* (New York: Simon and Schuster, 1995).
5. How could it be otherwise? Analytical work in anthropology has shown that human culture is basically the outcome of strategic interactions among participants in a culture (Robert Boyd and Peter Rich-

erson, *Culture and the Evolutionary Process* [Chicago: University of Chicago Press, 1985]). Those interactions can be stylized, written down, and even expressed in mathematical terms borrowed from biological theories of system evolution (Herbert Gintis, *Game Theory Evolving* [Princeton: Princeton University Press, 2000]). Stripped of all context, these bare-bones models can be shown to produce the core icons of a culture: shared symbolic meanings, languages, taboo, ritual, prestige, power. Similar work in political science, public policy, and sociology indicates that simple abstract models can be used to understand a dramatically wide variety of human social behavior (political science: William H. Riker, "Implications from the Disequilibrium of Majority Rule for the Study of Institutions," *American Political Science Review* 74 (1980): 432–446; public policy: Elinor Ostrom, Roy Gardner, and James Walker, *Rules, Games, and Common-Pool Resources* [Ann Arbor: University of Michigan Press, 1994]; sociology: James S. Coleman, *Foundations of Social Theory* [Cambridge: Harvard University Press, 1990]). The success of this approach in explaining how human society works has an implication that has never been noticed: If human sociality can indeed be described in the abstract, it follows that the human sociality we observe everyday will emerge wherever groups of humans congregate. Human sociality is a feature of humans, not of this Earth we live on. Thomas Malaby states that games are just a certain kind of process that humans engage in. There can be games in "reality" and games in "virtuality"; the real and the virtual are just two comparable arenas within which games can happen. Thomas Malaby, "Beyond Play: A New Approach to Games," *Social Science Research Network* (2006), http://papers.ssrn.com/sol3/papers.cfm?abstract_id= 922456.

6.   Julian Dibbell, *Play Money: Or, How I Quit My Day Job and Made Millions Trading Virtual Loot* (New York: Basic, 2006).

7.   Michael Vlahos, "Entering the Infosphere: Communication Network as Social and Political Space," *Journal of International Affairs* 51(2) (1998): 497–526. Jeffrey R. Cooper, "The CyberFrontier and America at the Turn of the 21st Century: Reopening Frederick Jackson Turner's Frontier," *First Monday* 5(7) (2000), http://www.firstmonday.org/issues/issue5_7/cooper/index.html.

8.   Richard A. Easterlin, "The Economics of Happiness," *Daedalus* 133(2) (2004): 26–33. Bruno Frey and Alois Stutzer, *Happiness and Economics: How the Economy and Institutions Affect Economic Well-Being* (Princeton: Princeton University Press, 2001). Daniel Kahneman, Ed Diener, and Norbert Schwarz, eds., *Well-Being: The Foundations of Hedonic Psychology* (New York: Russell Sage, 1999); Stefan Klein, *The Science of Happiness: How Our Brains Make Us Happy—and What We Can Do to Get Happier* (New York: Marlowe and Company, 2006/2002); Daniel Gilbert, *Stumbling on Happiness* (New York: Knopf, 2006); Mihaly Csikszentmi-

halyi, *Flow: The Psychology of Optimal Experience* (New York: Harper and Row, 1990).

9. "Games" and "play" are not the same thing. A game is a designed goal environment with an uncertain outcome. Play is anything that's not serious. The stock market is a game that's not play. A piece of code labeled "video game" may well be an extremely serious piece of interactive software.

CHAPTER TWO

1. Steven L. Kent, *The Ultimate History of Video Games: From Pong to Pokemon—The Story Behind the Craze That Touched Our Lives and Changed the World* (New York: Three Rivers, 2001).

2. Douglas Rushkoff, *Playing the Future: What We Can Learn From Digital Kids* (New York: Riverhead, 1996). Mark Pesce, *The Playful World: How Technology Is Transforming Our Imagination* (New York: Ballantine, 2000).

3. Dmitri Williams, "A Structural Analysis of Market Competition in the U.S. Home Video Game Industry," *International Journal on Media Management* 4(1) (2002): 41–54.

4. Byron Reeves and Clifford Nass, *The Media Equation: How People Treat Computers, Television, and New Media Like Real People and Places* (Cambridge: Cambridge University Press, 1996).

5. Annie Lang, "Using the Limited Capacity Model of Motivated Mediated Message Processing (LC4MP) to Design Effective Cancer Communication Messages," *Journal of Communication* 56 (2006): 1–24.

6. The context of these studies is individual experiments in labs. Subjects are exposed to a media environment, and physiological measurements of response, attention, and emotion are taken.

7. Example: In the United Kingdom, TV viewing is falling by about 2 percent per year in younger demographics. BBC News, "Fewer Young People Watching TV," observed August 2006 at http://news.bbc.co.uk/2/hi/entertainment/4758932.stm.

8. T. L. Taylor, *Play Between Worlds: Exploring Online Game Culture* (Cambridge: MIT Press, 2006).

9. Lawrence Lessig, *The Future of Ideas* (New York: Random House, 2001). To be specific about terms like "economically worthless": There can be no debate about the lack of economic worth to music distribution firms. Digitized music can be distributed at zero marginal cost. Information about what music to buy can be obtained through expertise aggregators, like DJs, who do it for free. There is no role in value chain for music distribution. That's the sense in which I mean "economically worthless." Music aggregators and distributors—publishers—are horse traders in a world that just invented cars. It surprises me that politicians are willing to establish long-running relationships with an industry that does not have a long run.

10. I thank Indiana University undergraduate student Tomas Feher for bringing this name to my attention.
11. Robert Dahl, *Democracy and Its Critics* (New Haven: Yale University Press, 1989).

CHAPTER THREE

1. Nicolas Ducheneaut, Nicholas Yee, Eric Nickell, and Robert J. Moore, "'Alone Together?' Exploring the Social Dynamics of Massively Multiplayer Online Games," *Xerox Palo Alto Research Center Working Paper,* observed May 2007 at http://www.parc.xerox.com/research/publications/files/5599.pdf.
2. S. Bardzell and J. Bardzell, Sex-Interface-Aesthetics: The Docile Avatars and Embodied Pixels of Second Life BDSM, *CHI 2006 World Conference on Human Factors in Computing Systems,* Montreal, Quebec, 2006.
3. "Videogame Boobs: A History," observed August 2006 at http://www.fleshbot.com/sex/videogames/videogame-boobs-a-history–176486.php.
4. Jane Pinckard, "Sex in Games: Rex + Vibrator," *Game Girl Advance* (October 26, 2002), observed May 2007 at http://www.gamegirladvance.com/archives/2002/10/26/sex_in_games_rezvibrator.html#000141.
5. Jane Pinckard, "Rez Trance Vibrator: Redux," *Game Girl Advance* (February 24, 2005), observed May 2007 at http://www.gamegirladvance.com/archives/2005/02/24/rez_trance_vibrator_redux.html.
6. Regina Lynn, "Ins and Outs of Teledildonics," *Wired News,* observed August 2006 at http://www.wired.com/news/culture/0,65064–0.html.
7. Daily Mail, "Downloads of Net Porn Hit Record High," observed August 2006 at http://www.dailymail.co.uk/pages/live/articles/news/news.html?in_article_id=388134&in_page_id=1770.
8. Greg Costikyan, "Death to the Game Industry (Long Live Games)," *Games * Design * Art * Culture* (July 28, 2005), observed May 2007 at http://www.costik.com/weblog/2005_07_01_blogchive.html#112254986073206098.

CHAPTER FOUR

1. Michael Vlahos, "Entering the Inforsphere: Communication Network as Social and Political Space," *Journal of International Affairs* 51(2) (1998), 497–526.
2. Frederick Jackson Turner, "The Significance of the Frontier in American History," *Proceedings of the State Historical Society of Wisconsin,* (1893).
3. Jeffrey R. Cooper, "The CyberFrontier and America at the Turn of the 21st Century: Reopening Frederick Jackson Turner's Frontier," *First Monday* 5(7) (2000), observed May 2007 at http://www.firstmonday.org/issues/issue5_7/cooper/index.html.

4. John R. Hicks, *The Theory of Wages* (London: Macmillan, 1932).
5. George J. Borjas, "Economics of Migration," *International Encyclopedia of the Social and Behavioral Sciences* (New York: Pergamon, 2000). Observed at http://ksghome.harvard.edu/~GBorjas/Papers/Migration_Encyclopedia_Article_Elsevier_Version.pdf.
6. Thomas H. Davenport and John C. Beck. *The Attention Economy: Understanding the New Currency of Business* (Cambridge: Harvard Business School Press, 2001).
7. Gary Becker, "A Theory of the Allocation of Time," *Economic Journal* 75(299) (1965), 493–517.
8. Becker, 493.
9. Becker, 517.

CHAPTER FIVE

1. For good surveys, see Ian Bogost, *Unit Operations: An Approach to Videogame Criticism* (Cambridge: MIT Press, 2006); Jesper Juul, *Half Real: Video Games Between Real Rules and Fictional Worlds* (Cambridge: MIT Press, 2005); Katie Salen and Eric Zimmerman, *Rules of Play: Game Design Fundamentals* (Cambridge: MIT Press, 2003).
2. Especially about ourselves. You should see some of the papers from my earlier career. Sleep aids!
3. There's even an evolutionary bias in favor of goals that have nothing to do with happiness. Edward Castronova, "Achievement Bias in the Evolution of Preferences," *Journal of Bio-Economics* 6(2) (2004): 195–226; Susan Blackmore, *The Meme Machine* (Oxford: Oxford University Press, 1999).
4. Robert Moffitt, "An Economic Model of Welfare Stigma," *American Economic Review* 73(5) (1983): 1023–1035.
5. A proper economic model of game playing would involve the idea of nested objective functions—the objective of the game being nested in an overarching objective function involving the usual arguments—income, status, consumption, and so on. Some work in this direction is provided by sports economists, especially those who study not the sports industry per se but the design of sports rules. See Stefan Szymanski, "The Economic Design of Sporting Contests," *Journal of Economic Literature* 41 (2003): 1137–1187.
6. Amartya Sen, "Welfare Economics and the Real World," *Acceptance paper for the Frank Seidman Distinguished Award in Political Economy* (Memphis, Tenn.: P.K. Seidman Foundation, 1986).

CHAPTER SIX

1. Raph Koster, *A Theory of Fun for Game Design* (Scottsdale, Ariz.: Paraglyph Press, 2005). Research on this subject has a longer history than

one might imagine; see Thomas W. Malone, "Heuristics For Designing Enjoyable User Interfaces: Lessons From Computer Games," Proceedings of the 1982 Conference on Human Factors in Computing Systems, 1982. This essay located the fun of playing games in three broad categories: challenge, fantasy, and curiosity. The devil is in the details, of course— what specifically are the mental states associated with these three categories, and how are they optimally tweaked?

2. Byron Reeves and Clifford Nass, *The Media Equation: How People Treat Computers, Television, and New Media Like Real People and Places* (New York: Cambridge University Press, 1996).

3. Annie Lang, "Using the Limited Capacity Model of Motivated Mediated Message Processing (LC4MP) to Design Effective Cancer Communication Messages," *Journal of Communication* 56 (2006): 1–24.

4. Annie Lang, "The Influence of Appetitive and Aversive Activation on the Processing of Video Games," in Paul Messarsis and Lee Humphries (eds.), *Digital Media: Transformation in Human Communication* (New York: Peter Lang Publishing, 2006), 237–56.

5. J. T. Caccioppo, W. L. Gardner, and G. G. Bernston, "The Affect System Has Parallel and Integrative Processing Components: Form Follows Function," *Journal of Personality and Social Psychology* 76(5) (1999): 839–855.

6. Daniel Kahneman, Ed Diener, and Norbert Schwarz (eds.), *Well-Being: The Foundations of Hedonic Psychology* (New York: Russell Sage, 1999).

7. Kahnemen, Diener, and Schwarz, p. xi.

8. T. Dalgleish, "The Emotional Brain," *Nature Reviews Neuroscience* 5 (2004): 583–9.

9. Stefan Klein, *The Science of Happiness: How Our Brains Make Us Happy—and What We Can Do to Get Happier* (New York: Marlowe and Company, 2006/2002).

10. Ed Diener, Richard E. Lucas, and Christie Napa Scollon, "Beyond the Hedonic Treadmill: Revising the Adaptation Theory of Well-Being," *American Psychologist* 61(4) (2006): 305–314.

11. Kent Berridge, "Simple Pleasures," observed August 2006 at http://www.apa.org/science/psa/sb-berridge.html.

12. Daniel Gilbert, *Stumbling on Happiness* (New York: Knopf, 2006).

13. Daniel Gilbert, "Here's to Tofu, Baseball, Heroin—and Dad!" observed August 2006 at http://www.randomhouse.com/kvpa/gilbert/blog/2006 06heres_to_tofu_baseball_heroin8.html.

14. Mihaly Csikszentmihalyi, *Flow: The Psychology of Optimal Experience* (New York: Harper and Row, 1990).

15. Johan Huizinga, *Homo Ludens* (Boston: Beacon Press, 1938/1950).

16. Francis Steen and Stephanie A. Owens, "Evolution's Pedagogy: An Adaptationist Model of Pretense and Entertainment," *Journal of Cognition and Culture* 1(4) (2001): 289–321.

17. Susan Blackmore, *The Meme Machine* (New York: Oxford University Press, 1999).

CHAPTER SEVEN

1. Richard Bartle, *Designing Virtual Worlds* (Indianapolis: New Riders, 2003), p. 702.
2. Lum is the inspiration for one of my own favorite online personae, whom I also refer to as "the Mad." With the boundaries between real and virtual wiggling like Jell-O, some level of madness seems only appropriate.

CHAPTER EIGHT

1. Robert H. Haveman, *Starting Even: An Equal Opportunity Program to Combat the Nation's New Poverty* (New York: Simon and Schuster, 1988).
2. John K. Galbraith, *The Affluent Society* (New York: Mariner, 1988/1958).
3. John Beck and Mitchell Wade, *Got Game: How the Gamer Generation Is Reshaping Business Forever* (Harvard Business School Press, 2004).
4. Here's how this actually happens: Every monster carries a small amount of money. Kill the monster, get the money. Thus any time a player needs money, he simply has to go out and start killing monsters. The system does not provide these funds by transferring money from some other source—it generates new money and injects it into the economy.

CHAPTER NINE

1. Jordan Peterson, *Maps of Meaning: The Architecture of Belief* (New York: Routledge, 1999).
2. Jean Baudrillard, *Simulacra and Simulation,* tr. Sheila Faria Glaser (1981; reprint Ann Arbor: University of Michigan Press, 1994); Joseph Campbell, *The Hero With A Thousand Faces* (1949; reprint Princeton: Princeton University Press, 1973); J. R. R. Tolkien, "On Fairy Stories," Andrew Lang Lecture, University of Edinburgh, 1939; available in *Tree and Leaf* (New York: Harper Collins, 2001).
3. Lawrence Lessig, *Code and Other Laws of Cyberspace* (New York: Basic, 1999).
4. Edward Castronova, *Synthetic Worlds* (Chicago: University of Chicago Press, 2005), p. 209.
5. A study by Dmitri Williams suggests that people who play violent video games for a long time come to believe that they are more likely to be attacked with weapons in the real world. Dmitri Williams, "Virtual Cultivation: Online Worlds, Offline Perceptions," *Journal of Communication* 56(1) (2006): 69–87.

CHAPTER TEN

1. Apparently quoted in Laurens van der Post, *Jung and the Story of Time.* See Charles Cameron, "Carl Gustav Jung on Game Design," observed

January 2007 at http://home.earthlink.net/~hipbone/IDTWeb/Why Game.html.

2. Richard Bartle, *Designing Virtual Worlds* (Indianapolis: New Riders, 2003) p. 702.

3. My therapist, John Ebling, M.S.W., served for 12 years as an emergency room social worker. He had, as he describes it, the "terrible privilege" of being with hundreds of people in their final hours. It would be interesting to see what sort of social order those people would collectively build if they had the chance in those last moments. I doubt that it would look much like the social order we live in today.

4. Stefan Klein, *The Science of Happiness* (New York: Marlowe and Company, 2006/2002).

5. Zeno Franco and Philip Zimbardo, "The Banality of Heroism," *Greater Good* (Fall/Winter) (2007), observed May 2007 at http://greatergood.berkeley.edu/greatergood/current_issue/francozimbardo.html.

6. These issues have been explored by many others. See, e.g., Sherry Turkle, *Life on the Screen: Identity in the Age of the Internet* (New York: Simon and Shuster, 1995), note 4.

7. See note 1.

8. Bruno Bettleheim, *The Uses of Enchantment* (New York: Vintage, 1977).

9. Jordan Peterson, *Maps of Meaning: The Architecture of Belief* (New York: Routledge, 1999).

10. Robert D. Putnam, *Bowling Alone: The Collapse and Revival of American Community* (New York: Simon and Schuster, 2000).

11. Humphrey Carpenter, *J.R.R. Tolkien: A Biography* (London: George Allen and Unwin, 1977).

12. J. R. R. Tolkien, "On Fairy Stories," Andrew Lang Lecture, University of Edinburgh, 1939; available in *Tree and Leaf* (New York: Harper Collins, 2001).

13. Susan E. Mayer, *What Money Can't Buy: Family Income and Children's Life Chances* (Cambridge: Harvard University Press, 1998).

EPILOGUE

1. Press Release observed May 2007 at http://clinton.senate.gov/news/statements/details.cfm?id=249860&&.

INDEX